THE
TRAVELLER'S
FRIEND

THE TRAVELLER'S FRIEND

Text compiled and written by Jennifer Barclay

Illustrations by Kath Walker

Summersdale Publishers Ltd
46 West Street
Chichester
West Sussex
PO19 1RP
UK

www.summersdale.com

Printed and bound by CPI Group (UK) Ltd, Croydon, CR0 4YY

ISBN: 978-1-84953-189-4

THE
TRAVELLER'S
FRIEND

A MISCELLANY OF
WIT AND WISDOM

ILLUSTRATIONS BY KATH WALKER

JENNIFER BARCLAY

summersdale

CONTENTS

INTRODUCTION

*Twenty years from now you will be more
disappointed by the things that you didn't do
than by the ones you did do. So throw off
the bowlines. Sail away from the safe harbour.
Catch the trade winds in your sails.
Explore. Dream. Discover.*

MARK TWAIN

It's been said many times and strikes a chord with all of us: no one on his death bed ever looked into the eyes of family and friends and said, 'I wish I'd spent more time at the office.' And it's rare you'll find anyone who regrets the time they spent travelling. I met a lady in western Canada once who was too old to travel long distances, who told me wistfully she had always wanted to go to Spain, and now she never would.

One of the joys of travel is that we're often learning something – either about history or culture or about ourselves, pushing our boundaries as we open up to new experiences. Sometimes we travel to escape a routine and give life a good shake, or to seek a change of climate or a change of pace. Some are looking for a place to stay, and end up living in voluntary exile, embracing the other world that offers something they needed – or embracing that special someone they fell in love with on their travels.

Whether you travel far or just around the corner, there's a wealth of new possibilities that makes it exciting. At the opening of *Yoga for People Who Can't be Bothered to Do It* by Geoff Dyer, he says he has been puzzled for years by lines from an Auden poem that talk about home as being the place where the three or four important things that happen to a man do happen. A lot of things have happened to him in a lot of different places, which form the basis of the compelling stories he tells. '"Home", by contrast, is the place where least has happened.'

When sometimes the adventure seems too challenging, it's worth remembering that it wasn't always so pleasurable or safe or easy to travel as it is largely today. Even in the world's most dangerous places, there's a fair chance of being able to let people know where you are. When we look back at the history of travel through the millennia, travel was for war and trade, and as in one of my favourite scenes from television's *Blackadder* where he is setting off on a voyage from Elizabethan England, the maps were still blank and had to be filled in.

But hearteningly, some of the most inspiring daredevil travellers featured in this book lived to a grand old age. And what stories they had to tell.

For some of us on this planet, the option of travel has been available for centuries. For others less fortunate, it is still an impossible dream. Let's value the beauty to be found when we roam, not spoil it, and by poking our noses into other cultures let's learn things about our own, and leave the world a place to be enjoyed by travellers to come.

*There is no end to the adventures we can have
if only we seek them with our eyes open.*

JAWAHARLAL NEHRU

*All my life I have felt that the wilderness
of the world is never that far away.*

CHRISTOPHER ONDAATJE

Why Travel?

There are certain views in all countries which must quicken the heart of the man who sees them again after an absence.

H. V. MORTON, *IN SEARCH OF SCOTLAND*

A TRAVELLER MAY BE...

A nomad, a wanderer, a tourist, a tripper, a journeyer, a jet-setter, a backpacker, a gadabout, a pilgrim, an explorer, a sightseer, a globetrotter, a gallivanter, a migrant, a rover, a drifter, a vagabond, a vacationer, a circumnavigator, a wayfarer...

Travel is always as much about where you go inside your head as where your feet take you.

CHARLES FORAN, *THE LAST HOUSE OF ULSTER*

Tread Softly

Until fairly recently in human history, travel was mainly for the sake of survival, whether to gain new territories through expansion and war, or to trade with others in commodities such as salt and spices to preserve food. People made voyages across terrifying oceans in ships built using skills we later lost. On land they travelled with camels, elephants and horses. The Phoenicians (from modern-day Lebanon) were already trading tin from as far afield as Britain and throughout the Mediterranean around 1000 BC. Two thousand years later, Norse explorer Eric the Red colonised Greenland, bringing 700 people as well as horses and cattle.

The Venetian Marco Polo came from a family of merchants involved in long-distance trading; his father was on expedition to China when he was born in 1254, and with his uncle they traded from Constantinople, then Crimea, then Uzbekistan. The Chinese emperor Kublai Khan asked them to be envoys to the pope and open up a sharing of civilisations. At seventeen, Marco Polo travelled through places then barely known to Europeans – Baghdad, Kashgar, the Gobi Desert – and the book he wrote about the Silk Road made it more widely known than ever before. His description of the wealth of the East inspired Christopher Columbus to try to reach it by sailing west – showing how travel books have changed our world.

The challenges of today are very different, with population growth and depleting resources. As Robert Kunzig reported in *National Geographic*, before the twentieth century 'no human had lived through a doubling of the human population, but there are people alive today who have seen it triple'. Because of advances in science, millions of people in developing countries who would previously have died in childhood survived to have children themselves, and although gradually family sizes will eventually diminish – people won't need to have so many children if they are all likely to survive – for now we have an astonishing spike in the global population. Meanwhile, 'water tables are falling, soil is eroding, glaciers are melting, and fish stocks are vanishing'. We are all aware of how our actions and choices may affect environmental change.

So, should we still travel?

Sara Wheeler, author of several travel books and two biographies, says she feels the damage caused by tourism and explorers is 'minuscule compared to the damage being done elsewhere'. Travel has always been a way of learning about the world, for the traveller and those he or she encounters. As Christopher Ondaatje said in an interview in *Traveller* magazine, 'I think the more knowledge you can bring to other people in the world, about what's happening, the better.'

*Travel is more than the seeing of sights;
it is a change that goes on, deep and
permanent, in the ideas of living.*

MIRIAM BEARD

*The best life is to be happy.
Happiness is travelling.*

NOMADIC QAANAAQ HUNTER IN GREENLAND, QUOTED IN GRETEL
EHRLICH'S *THIS COLD HEAVEN: SEVEN SEASONS IN GREENLAND*

THE ROAD TO NOWHERE:
TERRA INCOGNITA

*I love that sense of arriving someplace
and you don't know a thing about it
and it turns out to be really delightful.*

BILL BRYSON, INTERVIEWED IN *A SENSE OF PLACE*

The less a man knows at the start of such a journey as mine the better. All he needs is restless curiosity.

H. V. MORTON, *IN SEARCH OF SCOTLAND*

A good traveller has no fixed plans and is not intent on arriving.

LAO TZU

HERE BE DRAGONS

In 1993, a team from the University of Zaragoza discovered a small stone tablet covered with strange markings in a cave in the Navarra region of northern Spain. The stone was smaller than seven inches by five, and less than an inch thick. Over the following fifteen years, researchers looked into the meaning of its etched lines and squiggles and came to believe they showed features of a landscape – in other words, a map – from 13,660 years ago, perhaps the earliest of its kind ever found. Pilar Utrilla, one of the team, said 'Whoever made it sought to capture in stone the flow of the watercourses, the mountains outside the cave and the animals found in the area... Complete with herds of ibex marked on one of the mountains visible from the cave itself.'

Thirty years earlier, James Mellaart had been excavating the Neolithic site of Çatalhüyük in Anatolia when he came across a wall painting approximately nine feet long, which radiocarbon tests dated to 6200 BC, depicting a town plan matching the site of Çatalhüyük itself, a distinct 'beehive' design settlement, and an erupting twin-coned volcano behind the town. This was clearly another notable find in the history of maps.

During excavations of the ruined city of Ga–Sur at Nuzi, 200 miles north of the site of ancient Babylon or present-day Iraq, a clay map-tablet small enough to fit in the palm of a hand was found, probably dating from between 3800 and 2300 BC. This one was inscribed with two ranges of hills bisected by a watercourse and, crucially, writing and symbols identifying places and plots of land, perhaps around Mesopotamia and Lebanon. The Babylonians gradually created their own mathematical system of cartography, one of the earliest maps of the world being their Imago Mundi of the sixth century BC. From then on, maps became more commonplace throughout the ancient empires of Greece and Rome.

In Roman times, all parts of the known world were represented in relation to Rome; the medieval Mappa Mundi, now kept in Hereford cathedral, shows Jerusalem at the centre. Drawn on a sheet of vellum supported by an oak frame, with red and gold leaf for emphasis, the rivers and seas in blue or green, this British treasure dates to around AD 1290; over a thousand such maps survive from the period, created in studios by monks to disseminate knowledge to the illiterate masses. Its drawings illustrating marvels of the natural world are mostly accurate but with notable fanciful exceptions, such as an imagined people called the Phanesii with huge ears in which to wrap themselves against the cold, and the Sciapod, a being who sheltered himself from the heat of the sun with his huge foot.

The only known use of the phrase 'HC SVNT DRACONES', 'here be dragons', is from the Lenox Globe map from around AD 1503, and the dragons – around the east coast of Asia – may have been the komodo dragons of Indonesia.

INTO THE UNKNOWN

In 490 BC, the Carthaginians set off in sixty ships to undertake a voyage around Africa led by Hanno the Navigator, who recorded details of places he visited in a *periplus*. From the Ancient Greek word meaning a 'sailing around', a *periplus* was a document that listed the ports and coastal landmarks, with approximate intervening distances, that the captain of a vessel could expect to find along a shore. On his return to Carthage, Hanno hung his account of the journey in the temple of Baal Hammon, and the Greek translation of it helps us to interpret his route.

They sailed west to the Atlantic and eventually south. After passing a wide river mouth teeming with crocodiles and hippopotamuses, most likely the Senegal, they encountered 'wild men clad in the skins of beasts who threw stones and drove us off'. Leaving the Niger Delta, they saw a 'huge mountain of fire' with lava pouring into the sea – Mount Cameroon – and fierce creatures with shaggy hair called 'gorillas'; the use of the word, which comes from a local phrase meaning 'powerful animal that beats itself violently', shows the likelihood that he did in fact travel this far south, and was backed up by the later writings of Roman author and naturalist Pliny the Elder who confirmed gorilla pelts were on show in Carthage. Eventually, Hanno abandoned the plan of sailing right round Africa as it was further than he'd thought and they were running out of supplies. But the shape of Africa was now established.

A JOURNEY OF DISCOVERY

The works of Chinese historian Ma Tuan-lin include an extract from ancient official records of a traveller's tale from AD 499. This was the story of the Buddhist priest Hwui Shin (Hue Shen), who had made a long journey east across the Pacific to an unknown land in 458 and lived there several decades before returning home.

In the land he discovered, called Fu-sang, he reported that people lived in houses made of planks and used tree bark to make clothes as well as for writing. There was no warfare, but criminals were imprisoned for life. Hwui Shin and his band of missionaries travelled into the hills and mountains and found deserts and a huge canyon with its sides striped in different colours and a river winding among boulders at the bottom of it.

Could it have been North America? Some say Japan, others Mexico. His story was translated into English by Charles Leland in 1875. Historians say it is possible that a Chinese junk could have completed the journey across the Pacific using ocean currents.

ADAPTED FROM *DISCOVERIES THAT CHANGED THE WORLD*, RODNEY CASTLEDEN

Preparations

There is no moment of delight in any pilgrimage like the beginning of it.

Charles Dudley Warner

So there I am, splayed out, one leg on the floor and the other perched over the leg of the dining room table in a manner reminiscent of some snooker player preparing to pot a black.

Imagine it.

This is not some contortion to reach the salt. Nor is it some sort of bizarre sexual practice involving erotic foodstuffs. What I am actually doing is reading a map – or at least attempting to read one.

STEVE HAYWOOD, *NARROWBOAT DREAMS*

I have come to the Himba... to empty myself a little of Western thinking, my usual preparation for an expedition.

BENEDICT ALLEN, *THE SKELETON COAST*

PLANNING AN EXPEDITION

If travelling off the beaten track, do some research into your destination – especially its seasons and diseases – to determine the best time to travel months in advance. Find out if you will need a course of vaccinations, and keep a record of them. Often these will need to be staggered and many must be in your system months before you go. Logistics should also be organised long before the trip begins. Do you need any visas? Make sure you know and apply in plenty of time to allow for national holidays and other delays.

Will you have problems accessing money along the way? Look into this before you go and contact the embassy for help and advice.

The internet means helpful information from travellers can be shared easily but double-check against a reliable official source such as the Foreign and Commonwealth Office, especially when checking the safety of a political situation.

Know something of the local customs before you go so you can prepare what gifts and clothing you might want to take.

TRAVELLERS' TIPS – THINGS TO CONSIDER WHEN PREPARING FOR A LONG TRIP

✈   Take prescriptions for any medication you are carrying

✈   Learn a few words of the language

✈   Take a first aid and self-defence course

✈   Ensure your passport is valid for at least six months
     after your return date

✈   Arrange travel insurance to cover any planned activities

✈   Carry photocopies of important documents and leave copies
     at home, or scan them and email to a web-based account

✈   Carry a sleeping bag or inner sheet

✈   Pack a torch

✈ If carrying a backpack, consider getting a slash-proof wire mesh for it

✈ Know where your valuables are at all times, and don't wear expensive things

✈ Carry a few notes of low denomination for paying for small items, and to hand over if necessary

✈ Find out whether you'll be able to use your mobile phone; to use a local SIM may mean unlocking your phone and can take weeks. It may be cheaper and easier to buy local phone cards; keep your numbers somewhere safe and back up online

✈ More than 99 per cent of all overseas travellers make it home safely

When preparing to travel, lay out all your clothes and all your money. Then take half the clothes and twice the money.

SUSAN HELLER

Had we not let our insides be turned into a bacteriological laboratory and our skins into sieves with I know not how many inoculations?

MARCO PALLIS, *PEAKS AND LAMAS*

THE EARLY DAYS
OF MODERN TRAVEL

*According to the law of custom, and perhaps
of reason, foreign travel completes the
education of an English gentleman.*

EDWARD GIBBON

THE ALLURE OF TRAVEL

Robert Macfarlane, in *Mountains of the Mind*, reminds us that for centuries 'the unknown' held no allure in itself; 'the chief incentives for exploration were economic, political or egotistical ones'. But during the late 1700s an appetite for new experience emerged, via such remote regions as the Arctic and the deserts of Africa. The essayist William Duff in 1767 recommended 'exploring unbeaten tracks and making new discoveries' as an ideal of the Enlightenment.

[Timbuktu] isn't the prettiest city, an opinion that has been repeated by foreigners who have arrived with grand visions ever since 1828...

PETER GWIN, *NATIONAL GEOGRAPHIC*

THE GRAND TOUR

From the mid 1600s until the mid 1800s, aristocratic British gentlemen and wealthy northern Europeans often took a Grand Tour of southern Europe as part of their education, taking in the highlights of classical antiquity and the Renaissance over a trip lasting months or even years.

One of the earliest, the 'Collector' Earl of Arundel in 1613–14 toured through Italy as far as Naples, taking the future architect Inigo Jones as his guide or *cicerone*. In 1670, Roman Catholic priest Richard Lassels' *The Voyage of Italy* was published in Paris and then London, showing how 'an accomplished, consummate Traveller' could be stimulated intellectually and ethically by travel.

Twenty years later, John Locke's *An Essay Concerning Human Understanding* argued that a new environment offered fresh stimuli and thus an opportunity for knowledge: in other words, that travel can broaden the mind.

By the 1700s, it was felt that those fortunate enough to travel had a responsibility to recount their observations to society and Grand Tourists brought back art, books and cultural artefacts.

Gradually, as new rail and steamship routes made it easier and cheaper, such travel became scorned for being unadventurous. Even Americans and young women chaperoned by spinster aunts were taking the well-worn circuit.

A GLOBAL ADVENTURE

In 1870, French writer Jules Verne was going through a difficult patch. His father had died, the Franco-Prussian War was continuing and there was no money coming in from his science fiction. Then one afternoon in a cafe in Paris, while reading a newspaper, he had an idea for a completely different new book – an adventure novel. Recent technological innovations had opened up the potential not only for local travel but for actual circumnavigation of the globe: in just a couple of years the First Transcontinental Railroad in America was completed, the Indian railways were linked across the sub-continent and the Suez Canal was opened. It meant that anyone with the means could buy the tickets and travel around the world in reasonable comfort and safety. But could it be done in eighty days? To find out, people would have to buy his book and follow the adventures of Phileas Fogg of London, who accepts a wager to prove just that, with his new French valet Jean Passepartout. It is a story of missed connections and strange encounters, obstacles and misunderstandings, sure to entertain anyone who ever set out on a challenging adventure. There have been many adaptations and variations since then on the theme of 'around the world in eighty days', one of the better known in recent times being the television series by Michael Palin of Monty Python fame.

COOK'S TOURS

In 1841 Thomas Cook, a cabinet-maker and former Baptist preacher, took a group of 500 teetotallers on a 12-mile railway trip from Leicester to Loughborough to attend a temperance meeting, charging them just a shilling per person. Believing that working people's ordinary lives could be better if they drank less and became better educated, he had a flash of inspiration about 'the practicability of employing the great powers of railways and locomotion for the furtherance of this social reform'. He arranged more over the next three summers, all on behalf of temperance societies and Sunday schools.

In 1845 he set up his first commercial excursion and published a handbook of the journey to Liverpool; by 1851 he was promoting his tours to the Great Exhibition at Crystal Palace in London through *Cook's Exhibition Herald and Excursion Advertiser*, and by 1855 he escorted his first tourists through Belgium, Germany and France, then expanded into Switzerland and across the Alps into Italy. To cater to the middle-class tourists, he made arrangements with hotels and issued the 'circular note' to be used instead of money to pay for accommodation and meals – an early form of traveller's cheque.

Not content to rest on his laurels, he continued into North America and even up the Nile, and at the age of sixty-three he went on a tour of the world for almost eight months: by steamship to New York, by rail to San Francisco, Pacific steamer to Japan, then China, India and Cairo. While most of the party returned to London, Cook set off on an extended tour of Egypt and Palestine. From then on, he would offer a conducted world tour as well as tickets to independent travellers.

It was Thomas Cook's son, John Mason Cook, the more business-minded, who created overseas editions of *The Excursionist*, the newspaper started by his father, which would become known as *The Traveller's Gazette* and continued to be published until 1939. Both died in the 1890s leaving the business to John's three sons, who sold it in 1928 to the Belgian operators of the Orient Express. Having gone through many changes since then, the company Thomas Cook now has around 19,000 employees. What's more, the phrase 'Cook's Tour', is still used in British English to mean a brief or cursory guide to a subject or place, originating from the trips organised by Thomas Cook in the nineteenth century.

THE BIRTH OF THE GUIDEBOOK

It was German printer and bookseller Karl Baedeker's popular travel guides, established in 1829, which began the custom of rating places with one to four stars. English-language editions were published by James and Findlay Muirhead, who then set up the Blue Guides. During World War Two, Germany launched a series of air raids on English cities of historical importance featured in *Baedeker's Great Britain*, as revenge for British attacks on German cities including Berlin. The Nazi government commissioned publication of several travel guides of occupied regions. The Baedeker company's premises were destroyed themselves in a 1943 air raid, but the company was revived after the war.

THE WORST JOURNEY
IN THE WORLD

*Black bears rarely attack. But here's
the thing. Sometimes they do.*

BILL BRYSON, *A WALK IN THE WOODS*

I stopped trying to establish a firm floor under myself where there was none. We might die or we might live. Both were good.

GRETEL EHRLICH, *THIS COLD HEAVEN: SEVEN SEASONS IN GREENLAND*, WHEN THE ICE BREAKS UNDER THE SLED ON WHICH SHE IS TRAVELLING

I lost a bit of that second toe, but it was too long anyway.

ROSIE SWALE-POPE, WHO RAN AROUND THE WORLD

TRAVELLERS' TIPS – DEALING WITH LEECHES

Some species of leech – including those used in medicine for thousands of years – will attach to the skin to suck the blood, and release an anaesthetic to prevent the host from feeling it. They latch on using a sucker and usually after an hour they are full and detach, but they can be removed with a fingernail or other flat object slid sideways to break the seal of the suckers – first the oral sucker at the smaller end of the leech, then the rear one – and flicked away. The wound should be cleaned with soap and water, and bandaged or covered to prevent infection. Bleeding may continue for a few hours or longer, depending on the location of the bite, because of the anti-clotting enzyme the leech secretes into the blood, but is not dangerous. Avoid scratching the wound.

The only guaranteed method of preventing bites in leech-infested areas is to cover the skin. Some recommend removing leeches using salt, chilli or dry tobacco but these methods, and using a flame, cause the leech to regurgitate its stomach contents into the wound, which increases the risk of infection. Bacteria, viruses and parasites from previous blood sources can survive within a leech for months and may be retransmitted.

CORRUPTION AND CROCODILES

In *Congo Journey*, Redmond O'Hanlon describes how he met many challenges: corrupt military, malaria, cholera and ebola virus, man-eating crocodiles and snakes, leopards and gorillas. The Central African republic is one of the last frontiers of the world, one of the most difficult to explore and one of the most interesting, according to the Dorset-born author who was natural history editor of the *Times Literary Supplement* for fifteen years and is a fellow of the Royal Geographical Society.

I am quite an avid reader of ordeals,
life-threatening experiences, and harrowing
diaries of near escapes. I see Three Months
in a Rubber Dinghy! *and my*
hand leaps to the shelf.

PAUL THEROUX, INTERVIEWED IN *A SENSE OF PLACE*

INSPIRING TRAVELLER: COLONEL JOHN BLASHFORD-SNELL

'It would be uncomfortable: snakes, insects, heat, rain, jungle and swamp.'

(*TRAVELLER* MAGAZINE)

Affectionately known as 'Blashers', Colonel John Blashford-Snell has organised and led over 100 expeditions, including the first vehicle crossing of the Darien Gap in the early 1970s and navigating 2,700 miles of the Congo River – both with environmental, medical and scientific objectives.

His grandfather was a sea captain in Jersey, his father an army chaplain and his mother known for her care of wounded and orphaned wildlife. He was born in 1936 and after education at the Royal Military Academy, Sandhurst, he served in the army for thirty-seven years.

In 1968, Emperor Haile Selassie of Ethiopia invited the British Army to explore and make the first descent of the Blue Nile; he was commissioned to train the team and lead the expedition, which was a success. The following year, he and his colleagues formed The Scientific Exploration Society 'to foster and encourage scientific exploration worldwide'. From 1978 to 1980 he ran Operation Drake, organising such projects for young people from various countries. This was followed by the launch of Operation Raleigh, involving over 10,000 young men and women from fifty nations in challenges that would allow them to return home as pioneers intent on putting something back into their communities. He ran additional projects specifically for the disadvantaged and inner city youth.

He continues to lead scientific and aid-based ventures to remote parts of the world, especially in South America. He was awarded the MBE for his leadership of the Blue Nile expedition and the OBE for Operation Raleigh.

WHEN FIRST CLASS ISN'T AN OPTION...

At the age of nineteen George Orwell (1903–1950) whose real name was Eric Blair, went to serve with the Indian Imperial Police in Burma since his parents were not wealthy enough to send him to university. There he had a good job with plenty of responsibility but contracted dengue fever, and while on leave in England he determined to become a writer. In 1927 he settled in London and began exploring the slums, dressing like a tramp to experience how the poorest lived. A year later he moved to Paris and lived in Rue du Pot-de-Fer, taking advantage of the low cost of living and bohemian lifestyle to pen *Burmese Days* and begin publishing journalism. After falling ill and having all his money stolen from the lodging house, he took a series of menial jobs like dishwashing, all of which provided more material for what would become in 1933 his first book, *Down and Out in Paris and London*.

Poverty and the injustice of society would be an obsession in a lifetime of now classic works by the author, and it is clear why in the way he conjures the compelling eccentrics who lived around him in Paris. The book opens with the unkempt Madame Monce coming out onto the pavement to yell *'Salope!'* at a lodger on the third floor for squashing bugs on the wallpaper instead of throwing them out the window like everyone else. It is an environment of 'the sour reek of the refuse-carts', of 'leprous houses' in a state of collapse packed with a floating population of Poles, Arabs and Italians, underneath which were bistros 'where you could be drunk for the equivalent of a shilling'.

Delhi airport was... it was just taking the piss.

WILLIAM SUTCLIFFE, *ARE YOU EXPERIENCED?*

Being in a ship is being in a jail,
with the chance of being drowned.

SAMUEL JOHNSON

OFF THE RAILS

*Great European train stations
stir my wanderlust.*

RICK STEVES, *RICK STEVES' POSTCARDS FROM EUROPE*

LAYING TRACKS

Rick Steves, possibly America's most popular authority on travel in Europe, has said he loves to stand in a train station and watch as the destination board flips over every few minutes, revealing a tantalising list of destinations where one could be simply by hopping on the right train. Slow or fast, the train can be one of the most relaxing ways to travel, with room to spread out, walk up and down, while the landscape slips by: my first glimpse of the scale of Canada came on an overnight train journey from Toronto to the east coast. Or it can be a cultural experience, for example a ten-hour journey in China I'll never forget: the only ticket that had been available was the notorious 'hard seat' and even so other passengers hurled themselves through the windows to share the space, squeezing onto and even under the bench; the situation was redeemed as morning came, in a poignant moment when the family opposite offered us a pomegranate from their breakfast. As Paul Theroux has commented, a train in many countries is a 'cultural artefact' that represents the country, containing 'its citizens, their chickens, their children, their eating and sleeping habits' – or demonstrating its sleek precision and gentility as I have experienced in Japan. Train stations can be tiny outposts, or grand like St Pancras – or Leipzig Hauptbahnhof, which has 140 shops and a winter ice rink. Haydarpaşa, Istanbul, is a favourite of many, standing on a promontory jutting into the Eastern side of the Bosphorus.

*I travelled from King's Cross to
Berwick-on-Tweed in a sleeper
on the night-express for no other
reason than that I like to read in
bed and, at the same time, feel that
I am being rushed forward
at a tremendous speed.*

VICTOR CANNING, *EVERYMAN'S ENGLAND*

WHAT THE DICKENS...?

Charles Dickens lived and worked in France, Switzerland and Italy, and sailed by steamer to America and Canada. He travelled on trains through Europe, and in his writings he describes the types of passengers he meets, such as the Demented Traveller, as well as the sense of rushing in a train through landscapes and – 'bang' – through stations. In his essay 'The Calais Night Mail' he meets an English traveller who 'thinks it a quite unaccountable thing that they don't keep "London time" on a French railway'.

On a single track, sometimes carried on a narrow ledge excavated from the mountain side by men lowered from the top in baskets, overhanging ravines from 2,000 to 3,000 feet deep, the monster train snaked its way upwards, stopping sometimes in front of a few frame houses, at others where nothing was to be seen but a log cabin with a few Chinamen hanging about it, but where trails on the sides of the ravines pointed to a gold country above and below. So sharp and frequent are the curves on some parts of the ascent, that on looking out of the window one could seldom see more than a part of the train at once. At Cape Horn, where the track curves round the ledge of a precipice 2,500 feet in depth, it is correct to be frightened, and a fashion of holding the breath and shutting the eyes prevails, but my fears were reserved for the crossing of a trestle bridge over a very deep chasm, which is itself approached by a sharp curve. This bridge appeared to be overlapped by the cars so as to produce the effect of looking down directly into a wild gulch, with a torrent raging along it at an immense depth below.

ISABELLA BIRD, 'LAKE TAHOE'

THE SETTLE–CARLISLE LINE

The Settle–Carlisle railway line is one of England's most dramatically scenic, and Dent Station in Cumbria is Britain's highest mainline station, 1,150 feet above sea level. It first opened in 1877, and at its peak ninety trains a day would pass through, with cattle and coal among the cargo. Now you can sleep there, as its ticket offices have been renovated to provide accommodation for rent. Although the old snow fences were not always successful in keeping the wrong kind of snow off the tracks, the new solar-powered underfloor heating and Rayburn Aga ensure there's comfort to match the breathtaking scenery.

WWW.DENTSTATION.CO.UK

PADDINGTON BEAR

Paddington, the polite bear with the love of marmalade sandwiches and the aptitude for hard stares, came from Deepest Darkest Peru; according to his biography, he was orphaned after an earthquake, and brought up by his Aunt Lucy. But when she went to live in the Home for Retired Bears in Lima, she sent him to England, arranging for him to travel as a stowaway in a ship's lifeboat. He was found by Mr and Mrs Brown at Paddington station, wearing a tag saying 'Please Look After This Bear. Thank You' and sitting all alone on a battered suitcase; they christened him after the station and took him home to live with them at 32 Windsor Gardens.

Paddington first appeared in 1958 in the first of a series of books by Michael Bond, which have since been translated into thirty languages and sold more than 30 million copies worldwide. There is now a bronze statue of this classic fictional creation in Paddington station.

Even when the world's first proper line opened, the Liverpool and Manchester Railway on September 15, 1830, the top speed was a pretty damn fast 35 mph; much speedier than galloping horses (around 25 mph at full pelt) and obviously capable of sustaining this rate over a much longer distance... Doctors were consulted in advance of the official opening to ensure that eyes would not be damaged taking in scenery as carriages whizzed by and that there would be no problems with breathing at such heady speeds... With the brilliant engineer George Stephenson at the helm of the Arrow and the Duke of Wellington on board (the hero of Waterloo was by then prime minister), the Victorians were wowed as the locomotives set off from Manchester to Liverpool and moved across the landscape as though by magic along the 31-mile route. It must have been a triumphant sight, with steam and smoke billowing across the landscape... the day marked the start of 'railway mania'. Almost immediately, across the world there was great excitement at the potential offered by this fast new form of travel.

TOM CHESSHYRE, *TALES FROM THE FAST TRAINS*

FIVE OF THE BEST-LOVED
TRAIN JOURNEYS IN THE WORLD

✈ Béziers to Clermont-Ferrand, France: from the wine-growing coast up into the wilds of Aveyron and Roquefort country.

✈ Palace on Wheels, India: ride across the deserts of Rajasthan via the majestic cities of Udaipur, Jaisalmer and Jodhpur in a luxurious train decorated with local textiles.

✈ Glacier Express, Switzerland: from Zermatt to Davos or St Moritz via untouched mountain landscapes, 291 bridges, 91 tunnels, and the Oberalp Pass at 6,670 feet.

✈ Glasgow to Fort William and Mallaig: one of the loneliest landscapes in Britain, with red deer in the glens and views around Ben Nevis and across the Atlantic towards Skye.

✈ California Zephyr: this double-decker takes just over two days from Chicago to San Francisco with panoramic views of Nebraska, the Rockies, the snow-capped Sierra Nevadas and Salt Lake City.

Travellers' Tales

Long voyages, great lies.

ITALIAN PROVERB

Tour-writing is the very rage of the times... Every-one now describes the manners and customs of every county thro' which they pass...

JOHN BYNG, *RIDES ROUND BRITAIN*

GULLIVER'S TRAVELS

*G*ulliver's Travels, a classic work of English literature by Anglo-Irish writer Jonathan Swift, was first published in 1726 and has since been adapted many times for music, theatre and film. A parody of a traveller's tale describing adventures and misadventures in mythical worlds among people with unusual behaviour and philosophies, its full title is: *Travels into Several Remote Nations of the World, in Four Parts. By Lemuel Gulliver, First a Surgeon, and then a Captain of Several Ships.* The best-known part is the first, in which he sets out on a voyage and is shipwrecked in Lilliput and taken prisoner by people less than six inches tall. Subsequent voyages take him to Brobdingnag, Laputa, Balnibarbi, Luggnagg, Glubbdubdrib and Houyhnhnms – by way of some real places such as Japan, Amsterdam and Barbados.

TRAVELLERS' TIPS – TAKING THE PERFECT HOLIDAY SNAPS

In this age of instant information, it is hard to be surprised by well-known sights or iconic monuments; we already have a mental image of Machu Picchu or the Taj Mahal, even if we've never been there. Look for an unusual angle that will show it in a different light – or literally aim for a special light in early morning or evening. Avoid times when there are tourists about, unless including crowds is an intentional effect.

Photographs of people can be some of the most powerful and don't require expensive equipment. When taking close-up portraits, it's probably a good idea to make sure the person is happy for you to take their picture, and it will allow you time to get it right. (There are places where people will ask for money in exchange for this, and it's up to you to decide whether it's appropriate in the situation. If people you photograph ask you to send them a copy, it's a nice way of thanking them.) Avoid bright or patchy backgrounds that will distract the focus away from the subject, and focus on the eyes. An image of a lone person in the landscape or people in everyday surroundings going about their daily tasks can be especially evocative.

Learn a little about your camera; the more you practise, the easier it will be to know how to capture the perfect moment when you see it.

Her father loved me; oft invited me;
Still question'd me the story of my life,
From year to year, the battles, sieges, fortunes,
That I have passed.
I ran it through, even from my boyish days,
To the very moment that he bade me tell it;
Wherein I spake of most disastrous chances,
Of moving accidents by flood and field
Of hair-breadth scapes i' the imminent deadly breach,
Of being taken by the insolent foe
And sold to slavery, of my redemption thence
And portance in my travels' history:
Wherein of antres vast and deserts idle,
Rough quarries, rocks and hills whose heads touch heaven
It was my hint to speak,—such was the process;
And of the Cannibals that each other eat,
The Anthropophagi and men whose heads
Do grow beneath their shoulders. This to hear
Would Desdemona seriously incline:
But still the house-affairs would draw her thence:
Which ever as she could with haste dispatch,
She'd come again, and with a greedy ear
Devour up my discourse: which I observing,
Took once a pliant hour, and found good means
To draw from her a prayer of earnest heart

That I would all my pilgrimage dilate,
Whereof by parcels she had something heard,
But not intentively: I did consent,
And often did beguile her of her tears,
When I did speak of some distressful stroke
That my youth suffer'd. My story being done,
She gave me for my pains a world of sighs:
She swore, in faith, 'twas strange, 'twas passing strange,
'Twas pitiful, 'twas wondrous pitiful:
She wish'd she had not heard it, yet she wish'd
That heaven had made her such a man: she thank'd me,
And bade me, if I had a friend that loved her,
I should but teach him how to tell my story,
And that would woo her. Upon this hint I spake:
She loved me for the dangers I had pass'd,
And I loved her that she did pity them.
This only is the witchcraft I have used:
Here comes the lady; let her witness it.

WILLIAM SHAKESPEARE, *OTHELLO*

INSPIRING TRAVELLER:
SIR RICHARD FRANCIS BURTON

'I have often taken the drug [hashish] rather for curiosity to discover what its attractions might be, than for aught of pleasurable excitement I have ever experienced...'

Richard Burton was an ardent explorer of Arabic literature, culture and religion, and speaker of some twenty-nine languages. He was born in Torquay in 1821, though somewhat typically for a man who loved to create a mystique about himself, in his autobiography he falsely claimed to have been born in the family home at Barham House in Hertfordshire. The family travelled a lot in his early years, living in France and Italy. He went to Oxford University but resolved to leave without obtaining a degree, getting himself expelled, and 'fit for nothing but to be shot at for six pence a day' he enlisted in the army of the East India Company and embarked on a voyage to Bombay in 1842, studying Hindustani en route.

In the East he dedicated himself to learning the local languages and culture to the extent that he was accused by fellow soldiers of 'going native'. This enabled him to travel in disguise, working as a kind of spy, famously aiding the investigation of a brothel in Karachi. He wrote in scandalous detail about the sexual practices he encountered on his travels; he seemed to relish shocking the establishment. After returning home and writing his first book, he then undertook a Hajj to Mecca in disguise in 1853, one of his best-known achievements in an enormously colourful life, as well as bringing the *Kama Sutra* to publication in English, and journeying with John Hanning Speke as the first Europeans to visit the Great Lakes of Africa in search of the source of the Nile.

He died in 1890 in Trieste where he served as British consul; Burton was thought to have secretly converted to Islam, so the dean of Westminster declined to have him buried in Westminster Abbey, and instead he was buried in St Mary Magdalen's Roman Catholic Church at Mortlake, which was then a village on the outskirts of London, in a mausoleum in the form of an Eastern traveller's tent. In her biography *A Rage to Live*, Mary S. Lovell says it was modelled on one he had made for his and his wife Isabel's travels in Syria, tall enough for Burton, at five feet eleven inches, to stand up in. Strings of camel bells hang from the ceiling, attached to an electrical shaker designed to make them tinkle when the door is opened.

THE GREAT ESCAPE

'Travelling,' she sighed. 'So predictable.'
'What's wrong with travelling?'
'Avoiding reality more like.'

DAVID NICHOLLS, *ONE DAY*

*When you're travelling, you are
what you are right there and then.*

WILLIAM LEAST HEAT-MOON, AUTHOR OF
BLUE HIGHWAYS: A JOURNEY INTO AMERICA

It is so sweet to find oneself free from the stale civilization of Europe! Oh my dear ally, when you first spread your carpet in the midst of these eastern scenes, do think for a moment of those your fellow creatures that dwell in squares, and streets and even... in actual country houses; think of the people that are 'presenting their compliments', and 'requesting the honour', and 'much regretting', – of those that are pinioned at dinner tables, or stuck up in ball rooms, or cruelly planted in pews – ay, think of these, and so remembering how many poor devils are living in a state of utter respectability, and you will glory the more in your own delightful escape.

ALEXANDER WILLIAM KINGLAKE, *EOTHEN: OR, TRACES OF TRAVEL
BROUGHT HOME FROM THE EAST*

A WELL-EARNED BREAK

There are times in life when we need to 'get away from it all' – the stresses of modern life, of professional responsibility – and a long stint of travel is just what's needed to recharge the batteries. It's now so common that it even has a name: the 'gap year' and the 'grown-up gap year'. Elizabeth Gilbert's book *Eat, Pray, Love* became a word-of-mouth bestseller, chronicling a year of spending time in Italy, India and Indonesia as she learned to be herself again after realising she was unhappy in her marriage and experiencing the guilt of divorce. The feeling can sneak up on us at any time and for many reasons; it may be a milestone birthday, or a feeling of being stuck in a rut; during a recession, time out might be forced upon you by changes in the workplace. Now that it's unusual to remain in the same job for a lifetime, it is much more acceptable and less risky to escape for a while during a time of transition to another type of work or into retirement. Whatever the reason, the concept of escape can be a strong temptation...

I asked myself for the hundredth time, 'Why am I doing this?' But I knew the answer. I was fifty-two, and I needed a change.

JILL LOWE, *YADAV: FINDING THE HEART OF INDIA*

I had come to Spitsbergen because that was where my old flame and good friend Edwin just happened to be living. He threw me Spitsbergen as a lifeline, a place to regroup and recover from the stress of my failed marriage. It could just as easily have been Borneo.

MARIE TIÈCHE, *CHAMPAGNE AND POLAR BEARS*

JOURNEY

A journey originally was no longer than a day. The Latin *diurnus*, 'of one day', evolved in Old French into *journée* meaning a day's work or travel; in French it now means simply 'day', but English took the other strand of meaning and by the early thirteenth century, it had been assimilated into English as 'a defined course of travelling', and in 1755 was still defined by Johnson as 'the travel of a day'.

Despite my homesick thoughts I knew that I was doing the right thing. I was twenty-five years old, single, and looking for a challenge. Paris had become dull and faded. It was time for something, somewhere, new.

ALEC LE SUEUR, *THE HOTEL ON THE ROOF OF THE WORLD: FIVE YEARS IN TIBET*

OUT OF DENMARK

Karen Blixen, born in 1885 in Denmark, wrote once to a friend that the Danish character was like 'dough without leavening'. It was Africa that provided the freedom that she found essential to happiness. She first went to Kenya with her husband Bror at the age of twenty-eight, and they started a coffee plantation; after contracting syphilis from him, and after meeting an English hunter, she finally separated from Bror, and took over the farm. She went on safaris in the bush and helped the local people in their daily lives, lobbying for schooling for indigenous people and eventually opening a school on her own property to teach them herself. 'I have become what I was meant to be here,' said the pioneer woman who had reinvented herself as Isak Dinesen, the name she used for her book *Out of Africa*. Isak in Hebrew means 'the one who laughs'.

ADDICTED TO TRAVEL

*Four hoarse blasts of a ship's whistle still
raise the hair on my neck and
set my feet to tapping.*

JOHN STEINBECK, *TRAVELS WITH CHARLEY*

The charm of West Africa is a painful one: it gives you pleasure when you are out there, but when you are back here it gives you pain by calling you. It sends up before your eyes a vision of a wall of dancing white, rainbow-gemmed surf playing on a shore of yellow sand before an audience of stately coco palms; or of a great mangrove-watered bronze river; or of a vast aisle in some forest cathedral: and you hear, nearer to you than the voices of the people round, nearer than the roar of the city traffic, the sound of the surf that is breaking on the shore down there, and the sound of the wind talking on the hard palm leaves and the thump of the natives' tom-toms; or the cry of the parrots passing over the mangrove swamps in the evening time; or the sweet, long, mellow whistle of the plantain warblers calling up the dawn; and everything that is round you grows poor and thin in the face of the vision, and you want to go back to the Coast that is calling you, saying, as the African says to the departing soul of his dying friend, 'Come back, come back, this is your home.'

MARY KINGSLEY, *TRAVELS IN WEST AFRICA*

*I travel a lot; I hate having
my life disrupted by routine.*

CASKIE STINNETT

*For my part, I travel not to go anywhere,
but to go. I travel for travel's sake.
The great affair is to move.*

ROBERT LOUIS STEVENSON

INSPIRING TRAVELLER: ISABELLA BIRD

'There never was anybody who had adventures as well as Miss Bird.'

THE SPECTATOR

Isabella Lucy Bird was born in 1831 and as the daughter of a priest she moved around Britain several times as he was sent to new parishes. She succumbed to illness often and at the age of nineteen she had a tumour removed from her spine, the operation leaving her prone to depression; but it has been noted that she was rarely ill when travelling.

In her early twenties, given £100 by her father to spend as she liked, she stayed with relatives in America and published her first book, *The Englishwoman in America*, then travelled to Canada. Already enamoured of travel, she decided to write books to support herself; although she had no desire to stay at home like her sister, she wrote her long letters, which formed the basis of her books, in which she increasingly aimed to present a clear view of societies still barely understood in Britain.

Her peregrinations took her all over North America, Asia and the Middle East, but certain extraordinary highlights are worth recounting. Having recently turned forty, she was on a ship to New Zealand when she decided to disembark at Hawaii, where she climbed the volcanic peaks and learned how to ride a horse astride, ending the backaches she had suffered riding side-saddle. She rode thus through the Rocky Mountains in Colorado, spent several months snowed in with two men in a cabin, and made the acquaintance of outlaw Jim Nugent. After a brief marriage to a doctor which ended in his death, she studied medicine and travelled to India at the age of sixty as a missionary. After crossing Tibet, she joined a group of British soldiers travelling between Baghdad and Tehran, armed with a revolver and a medicine chest. She met with British Prime Minister William Gladstone to speak out against atrocities being committed against the Armenians under the Ottoman sultan. In China she was attacked as a 'foreign devil' by people who had never seen westerners and was trapped in a burning house.

It was while planning another trip to China that she died in Edinburgh just before her seventy-third birthday. Author of sixteen books, frequently appearing in journals and magazines, Isabella Bird was a celebrity in her day; a lifelong traveller, she was the first woman inducted into the Royal Geographical Society.

15 TRAVEL TUNES

'Like a Rolling Stone' – Bob Dylan
'Leaving on a Jet Plane' – John Denver
'Back in the USSR' – The Beatles
'Born to be Wild' – Steppenwolf
'Road to Nowhere' – Talking Heads
'Come Fly With Me' – Frank Sinatra
'Never Let Me Down Again' – Depeche Mode
'Wish You Were Here' – Pink Floyd
'Come Away With Me' – Norah Jones
'Time to Move On' – Tom Petty
'Sail Away' – David Gray
'Home for a Rest' – Spirit of the West
'Graceland' – Paul Simon
'Life is a Highway' – Tom Cochrane
'King of the Road' – Roger Miller

TRAVELLERS' CLUBS

Royal Geographical Society, founded 1830 – former haunt of Sir Richard Burton and David Livingstone; houses an Expedition Advisory Centre and a collection of journals and maps.

The Explorers Club, founded 1904 – membership devoted to scientific adventures around the world; taste scorpions and rattlesnake at its annual exotic-foods dinner.

Royal Over-Seas League, founded 1910 – a Commonwealth membership organisation to foster international understanding and friendship.

The Adventurers Club, founded 1911 – for mountain climbers, polar adventurers and big-game hunters; recommendation required to join.

Travelers' Century Club, founded 1954 – for those who have travelled to a hundred countries or more; membership brings bragging rights, speakers and newsletters.

The Frontline Club – founded 2003 by a legendary freelance combat cameraman, its membership includes the most intrepid journalists and photographers of war zones.

JOBS YOU MIGHT WANT TO CONSIDER IF YOU'RE TRULY ADDICTED TO TRAVEL

Travel writer
Tour guide, wilderness guide
Massage therapist/yoga instructor
Chef
Bartender
Cabin crew
Teacher of English as a foreign language (or other language)
Volunteering
Long-haul trucker
Circus performer
Surf instructor
Hotel staff
Musician

A Taste for Foreign Parts

Although some foreigners claim to like yak butter tea they cannot possibly be telling the truth. They say that it is an 'acquired taste' but what deprivations you have to undergo to acquire the taste they do not say.

ALEC LE SUEUR, *THE HOTEL ON THE ROOF OF THE WORLD: FIVE YEARS IN TIBET*

*The only food she ever declined was the eye
of a roast sheep: she wasn't sure, she
said afterwards, whether it would
scrunch or squelch.*

MILES CLARK, WRITING OF BERYL SMEETON IN *HIGH ENDEAVOURS*

*Foreigners cannot enjoy our food, I suppose,
any more than we can enjoy theirs. It is not
strange; for tastes are made, not born. I might
glorify my bill of fare until I was tired; but
after all, the Scotchman would shake his head,
and say, 'Where's your haggis?' and the Fijian
would sigh and say, 'Where's your missionary?'*

MARK TWAIN, *A TRAMP ABROAD*

GASTRONOMIC ADVENTURES

The way to a traveller's heart is through his or her stomach, perhaps... When we fall in love with a culture, very often we fall in love also with the food. And we can revisit the place through its recipes. At the beginning of Elizabeth Gilbert's *Eat, Pray, Love*, she is eating ice cream in Italy, and she makes a conscious effort to indulge herself during her time there in foods that simply make her happy. But it's unlikely we'll fall for everything: there's always going to be something that's a challenge. In Elizabeth Bard's *Lunch in Paris*, it's *andouillette* – the strong-smelling tripe and chitterlings sausage – that will test her new affiliation with France. The website www.weird-food.com documents a lot of examples. As they say, 'Every culture invents a food that is weird or disgusting to outsiders.' There you will find recipes for banana worm bread and chocolate cricket cookies. Cambodia must take a lot of credit for eating fried spiders, and South East Asia has a good laugh over durian fruit, which are actually banned because of their smell in many countries, but Sweden might be number one with *surströmming*, herring left in a barrel to ferment for a few months until it smells so bad it has to be eaten outdoors.

A NICE CUP OF TEA AND A SIT DOWN

Just after a landmark birthday, Alan Whelan set out to ride a motorcycle from his home in Lancashire to Cape Town, where his wife comes from, answering the call of the continent. He had an unusual quest, however: to sit down and have a cup of tea with people along the way. Tea-drinking being a democratic ritual, he found himself sharing a cuppa with an amazing variety of people. In north-western Nigeria on a lonely stretch of road, desperately searching for a place to stay the night, he arrived in a dark village where he was invited to stay at the home of the local pastor. Many of the villagers had never seen a white man before. In the morning, they held a tea party for him. It's one of many memorable tea encounters related in his book *African Brew-Ha-Ha*. 'I think of the welcome the previous evening, the shower, the meal, the bedroom prepared specially, and everybody who came to welcome me and feel a lump coming to my throat.'

One of the minor peculiarities of an Indian tour is the sheer hopelessness that attends any search for a drinkable cup of tea.

MARCO PALLIS, *PEAKS AND LAMAS*

*Food is a central activity of mankind,
and one of the single most significant
trademarks of a culture.*

MARK KURLANSKY

In fact, *cocido* is a selection of slow-cooked, pot-boiled meats. Everything that was in the pot is served: whole chorizo sausages, potatoes, chickpeas, *grelos,* a slab of veal (for variety), plus a great deal of pig. The main attraction is *lacón,* the shoulder (foreleg) ham, but then there's belly, hock (ankle), snout, cheek, armpit... Traditionally, these would be all the parts of the animal that were preserved in salt when the pig was slaughtered during the onset of winter, and which could be used in stews throughout the winter, when there was nothing much else to eat.

To say *cocido* is unsophisticated is to miss the point.

JOHN BARLOW, *EVERYTHING BUT THE SQUEAL:
A YEAR OF PIGGING OUT IN NORTHERN SPAIN*

'French food is seen as the best in the world. The French, they have one hundred and seventy different cuts of the cow, of beef. Koreans, we have more than two hundred. Close to three hundred.'

An impressive fact, although I wonder privately if it is a good thing to eat that many parts of a cow.

JENNIFER BARCLAY, *MEETING MR KIM*

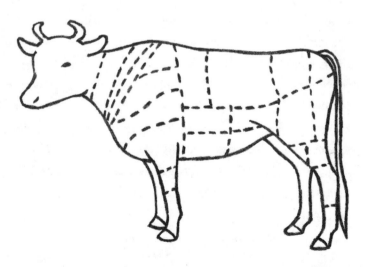

Platters are placed on the table: slices of wild-boar salami, tiny spicy venison sausages, rounds of toast topped with coarse chicken-liver pâté sweetened with Marsala, shiny black olives tossed in garlic and parsley. Wine is tipped into glasses and wedges of crusty spongy bread passed around. Lunch has begun.

Pasta comes next, a deep ceramic bowl of steaming spaghetti in a simple tomato sauce fragrant with fresh basil, or a rich cream redolent of wild mushrooms. On top of the fire have been placed two metal grills, which clip together to enclose the main course: thick slabs of prime beef, a handful of quails, fat home-made sausages. Passed around the table they are black-striped and crisp from the flames, perfumed with fresh rosemary, garlic and good oil.

Afterwards there is a chunk of Parmesan, aged and crumbly, and a tangy pecorino from Sardinia to eat with a large bowl of various fruits. This is the winding-down stage of the lunch, when women begin to push back chairs and carry out plates and men light up cigarettes and pour whisky. Coffee brews aromatic from the kitchen, conversation subdues, becomes sleepy, comfortable and confidential. Pastries accompany the coffee: a wealth of shortbreads, crunchy almond biscuits, macaroons and iced eclairs bulging cream. Vin Santo sweet and dark is poured into small glasses; outside the evening has begun to descend, and Sunday lunch settles.

Victoria Cosford, *Amore and Amaretti:*
A Tale of Love and Food in Italy

MARKETS

In a strange town, what better way to connect with the local culture than visiting the market? It will most likely be in an old and central part of town. There you will see how the locals live and sample what they eat, probably quite cheaply and more authentic than at a restaurant. You may even get into conversation with a shopper or stallholder, and you'll almost certainly get some great photographs. Just look out for pickpockets and other scams: even if crime is uncommon there, thieves often look for prey in the markets. Here are some interesting markets:

Psar Kandal Market, Phnom Penh, Cambodia
Banana flowers, fresh chillies and mangoes, fish in tanks and preserved eggs of all sizes and colours, all displayed in baskets.

Old Market Hall, Helsinki, Finland
Reindeer slices, Arctic cloudberries and pickled herring, overlooking the South Harbour: some seafood vendors sell direct from their boats.

Mercado Central, Alicante, Spain
Gothic building with colourful vegetables, melt-in-the-mouth pastries, fine Serrano ham, fish on ice, and a flower market.

Doncaster Market, England

In the heart of town since medieval times, with over 400 stalls including pie makers and a hot roast deli, Italian pizza and Greek delicatessen, fresh fish and game.

Granville Island Public Market, Vancouver, Canada

Locally grown tomatoes and fiddleheads, salmon jerky, Asian spices and bull kelp, exotic teas and Okanagan wines, all spectacularly oceanside.

Brixton Market, London, England

Caribbean salt fish and jerk chicken, Brazilian sausages, coffee shops and bakeries, in a multicultural atmosphere; prices put Borough Market to shame.

Isle sur la Sorgue, Provence, France

On a Sunday, the whole town and its canals are taken over by fresh seasonal produce and antiques; stay for the post-market lunch when everyone repairs to cafes.

Neighbourhood Goods Market, Cape Town, South Africa

Everything organic, farm-fresh and eco-friendly, housed in a Victorian warehouse at the Old Biscuit Mill; chutneys, pastries, biltong and beer.

English Market, Cork, Ireland

Looks more Spanish than English, but older than Barcelona's Boqueria. Locally made cheese, butter and bread, fresh-caught and smoked fish.

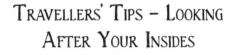

Travellers' Tips – Looking After Your Insides

To avoid diarrhoea, or 'Delhi Belly', eat at busy places where food is freshly prepared, not buffets where it could have been sitting around for hours. Avoid salads, cocktails, ice cream and ice. If you suspect you may have a bug, take in fluids and eat dry crackers.

Carry salt on your travels. It will replenish lost salt in a hot climate. A salt solution will help fight off a sore throat or mouth infection. Hot salty water is good for healing.

You Can't Take it With You

He who would travel happily must travel light.

Antoine de Saint-Exupéry

One remembers several evenings standing knee-deep in the debris of packing...

Marco Pallis, *Peaks and Lamas*

Let your memory be your travel bag.

Alexander Solzhenitsyn

THE THINGS THEY CARRIED

Quite apart from the cerebral baggage we may take on our travels, how much do we need to pack? While the famous Phileas Fogg and his valet Jean Passepartout in Jules Verne's *Around the World in Eighty Days* took only a carpet bag with two shirts and three pairs of stockings each, a mackintosh, a travelling cloak and a spare pair of shoes as well as a guide to the timetables of trains and steamers, Fogg also took twenty thousand pounds, which must have helped. Victorian travellers in general 'had no conception of travelling light', as Nicholas Murray points out in *A Corkscrew is Most Useful: The Travellers of Empire*; he tells of the traveller who required twelve camels to transport her, a female travelling companion and her baggage. Is it always women who want to squeeze more into their luggage? At the start of *Are We Nearly There Yet?* by Ben Hatch, in which he describes travelling around Britain for several months in a small car with his entire family, the opening scene centres around whether or not his wife Dinah may have sneaked an extra pair of shoes into the car when Ben wasn't looking. Writer and TV presenter Giles Coren counts among his pet hates, however, the unmanly trend among men to use wheelie luggage: 'minuscule bags on wheels scampering along behind them at the end of a long stick like some rectangular Chihuahua.'

I carried the basic minimum, including a tent that eliminated the need to look for lodgings at nightfall. This gives you a comforting sense of independence.

JOHN HILLABY, *JOURNEY THROUGH BRITAIN*

I travel with one carry-on-sized bag and never check it when I fly.

PAUL THEROUX

Medical Kit Checklist:

First aid manual
Antiseptic cream/wipes
Plasters, roll of bandage and safety pins, gauze strips
Scissors
Anti-diarrhoea tablets
Painkillers
Water-purifying tablets
Insect repellent
Sunscreen

*Good company in a journey
makes the way seem shorter.*

Izaak Walton

Lost in Translation

*He that travelleth into a country before he
hath some entrance into the Language,
goeth to school, and not to travel.*

Francis Bacon

The reward for trying lies in the possibility of a real exchange of thoughts... one of the greatest joys of travel.

Marco Pallis, *Peaks and Lamas*

ON LEARNING THE LANGUAGE

The nineteenth-century traveller needn't fear being misunderstood on the Continent, as long as he or she were equipped with a copy of *A Handbook of Travel-Talk: Being A Collection of Questions, Phrases, and Vocabularies, In English, German, French, and Italian; Intended to Serve as Interpreter To English Travellers Abroad, Or Foreigners Visiting England.* This handy tome provided translations to such essential phrases as:

Would you be so kind as to pass me the vinegar-cruet?
Fetch me some Windsor soap and a towel.
Lace my stays.
I want an elegant carriage for driving in the town.
You must have some leeches put on.

Pleased to Meet You

Shaking hands as a custom of greeting arrived in Fiji in the nineteenth century, and was embraced enthusiastically; a friendly handshake can be very long, and may even last throughout an entire conversation. In Morocco, you shake hands with your right hand then touch your hand to your heart. Shaking hands across a threshold is considered unlucky in Russia. There are many different rules of etiquette around the world for shaking hands, but remember that the left hand is considered unclean in some cultures.

MAKING FRIENDS

'A journey is best measured in friends, rather than miles,' said Tim Cahill. So you're going to need a few words of the language. 'Please' and 'thank you' in the local tongue accompanied by a smile will get you a welcome more often than not.

But what if you want to get to know someone a little better? A foreign accent can be charming – to them as well as to you. So you may want to take a few tips from Jake Harris's *Little Book of Essential Foreign Chat-up Lines*; even if what you're saying is ridiculous, you never know, someone may give you credit for trying to break the ice! Well, on second thoughts, maybe it's best to stick to the phrasebook instead...

When God made you, he was showing off.
FRENCH: *Quand Dieu t'a créée, il s'est surpassé!*

You've got a smile that could light up a whole town.
ITALIAN: *Il tuo sorriso potrebbe illuminare una città intera.*

Can I take your photo, so I can show Santa what
I'd like for Christmas?
GERMAN: *Ich brauche dein Foto, damit der Weihnachtsmann
weiss, was ich mir wünsche.*

It's my birthday – how about a birthday kiss?
SPANISH: *Es mi cumple, ¿qué tal un besito de cumpleaños?*

HOW TO SOUND LIKE A NATIVE IN FRANCE

If someone asks you a question, you are not obliged to formulate a coherent reply: you can simply respond by shrugging your shoulders, raising your eyebrows and uttering *'Bof'*.

Finish every sentence with *'quoi'*.

Call McDonald's *'McDo'*.

When you're posing for a photograph, don't say 'cheese'. Don't say *'fromage'* either, but *'ouistiti'*. It means marmoset.

Wish people well in whatever they are doing, whether having a meal *(Bon appétit)*, having a nice day *(Bonne journée)*, having a good journey home *(Bonne route)*, finding their way into a hotel room *(Bonne installation)*, doing their laundry *(Bon lavage)* or whatever they may happen to be doing at the time – and which you wish them to continue to enjoy doing *(Bonne continuation)*.

'Sorry, who are you?'

'Me? Oh, I friend of Miguel.'

'And who is Miguel when he's at home?'

'Miguel is friend of Joan who is brother of Jaume'.

The genealogy lesson doesn't stop here. 'Jaume's grandfather was doctor.'

I resist the childish urge to say, 'Doctor Who?' and instead ask, 'So who is Jaume?'

He looks bemused and shrugs his lean brown shoulders.

'Jaume is builder. Jaume work on your house.'

ANNA NICHOLAS, *A LIZARD IN MY LUGGAGE*

Ocean Roads

When you travel by boat be prepared to swim.

<small>CHINESE PROVERB</small>

INSPIRING TRAVELLERS: MILES AND BERYL SMEETON

'Ours was the fate of the restless wanderer, the skyline is never an end but only a bound...'

THE MISTY ISLANDS

This couple were pioneers of a nomadic ocean-cruising lifestyle. Miles was born in Yorkshire in 1906, and went to the Royal Military Academy at Sandhurst; Beryl came from a family of soldiers also. In the 1930s, Beryl travelled alone on four continents by road, river and rail, foot and horseback. They married in 1938, and the following year they climbed to 23,000 feet in the Himalaya with Sherpa Tenzing Norgay: the greatest height ever climbed by a woman at the time.

After World War Two, during which Miles served in Africa and was awarded the Distinguished Service Order in Burma, they settled on an island farm off the west coast of Canada with their daughter Clio. A few years later, unable to transfer some money from England, they instead bought the ketch *Tzu Hang* there and, teaching themselves to sail along the way, sailed back via the Panama Canal. In their fifties, they sold the farm and sailed for Australia. Returning from there via Cape Horn to England with a friend to visit Clio at school, they were hit by a rogue wave and Beryl was tossed overboard, the boat severely damaged. They managed to sail it to Chile to be repaired, but the following year hit storms again. The experiences provided material for their classic sailing book *Once is Enough*, and didn't dissuade them from further voyages. For twenty years they sailed the world. Biographer Miles Clark wrote in *High Endeavours* that Miles 'once confided that between them Beryl and he had travelled across every page of *The Times Atlas of the World*'.

At last they settled in the foothills of the Canadian Rockies and devoted the last twenty years of their lives to breeding endangered species of wildlife. Their books, written years after the events took place, include *The Sea Was Our Village* and Beryl's *The Stars My Blanket* describing her pre-war thousand-mile trek on horseback in the Andes and a hike through the jungles of Burma and Thailand. Beryl died in 1979 and Miles in 1988.

Miles said Beryl's love of adventure never left her: 'If a flying saucer landed in front of us and an insect hand beckoned us on board, she would step inside without hesitation...'

*The mildest-tempered people, when on land,
become violent and bloodthirsty
when in a boat.*

JEROME K. JEROME, *THREE MEN IN A BOAT*

*I relished the sound of 'seafarer'... It rolled
around my tongue and tasted of history.*

DAVE CLARKE, *AN OCEAN AWAY*, ABOUT SAILING SINGLE-HANDEDLY
ACROSS THE ATLANTIC; HE THEN ROWED SOLO ACROSS THE ATLANTIC,
BECOMING THE FIRST PERSON TO DO BOTH

Serious Adventurers Only

In 2011, Anthony Smith celebrated his eighty-fifth birthday halfway through a sixty-six-day transatlantic voyage of almost 3,000 miles on a sail-powered raft made of water pipes. 'Some people say it was mad. But it wasn't mad. What else do you do when you get on in years?'

Smith, an explorer, best-selling science writer and former television presenter was no stranger to adventure, having been the first Briton to cross the Alps in a balloon. He put an ad in *The Daily Telegraph*:

'Fancy rafting across the Atlantic? Famous traveller requires 3 crew. Must be OAP. Serious adventurers only.' He received hundreds of eager responses.

A whale played alongside the raft one day, and a school of mahimahi followed the raft almost the entire journey. 'The wildlife was just fantastic,' said crew member John Russell. 'There is nothing to be scared of. We were all old men.' Another crew member Andrew Bainbridge baked Smith a birthday cake on board.

The four-man crew wanted to prove the elderly are capable of embarking on adventures that are mistakenly considered dangerous. They also aimed to raise money for the British non-profit group WaterAid, which provides potable water to impoverished communities.

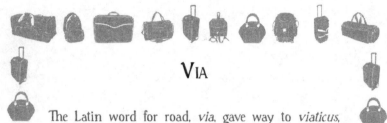

VIA

The Latin word for road, *via*, gave way to *viaticus*, meaning 'of or for a journey', the provisions for travel. Gradually *viaticum* came to mean the journey itself, and from this came the Old French *veiage* meaning 'travel, journey' around the year 1300 – the derivation of our modern word voyage.

LIFE ON THE WAVES

'The proudest moments of my life have been passed in the stern-sheets of a boat,' wrote author Robert Louis Stevenson, who sailed in 1888 with his family from San Francisco to wander the islands of the South Pacific to restore his bad health. He spent time in Hawaii, the Marquesas and the Gilbert Islands, Tahiti and Samoa. His wife Fanny published a journal of one of their voyages, *The Cruise of the Janet Nichol*. In 1890 he purchased land on one of the Samoan islands and lived there to the end of his days, known in the local language as Tusitala, the 'teller of tales', helping the Samoans and getting involved in politics. Frustrated by his continuing bad health, he determined to live his last years to the full. He died there, aged forty-four, and was buried overlooking the sea, having requested the following be inscribed on his grave:

Under the wide and starry sky,
Dig the grave and let me lie.
Glad did I live and gladly die,
And I laid me down with a will.
This be the verse you grave for me:
Here he lies where he longed to be;
Home is the sailor, home from sea,
And the hunter home from the hill.

*There is something satisfyingly eerie
about a landfall – any landfall.*

JONATHAN RABAN, *COASTING*

*Nowhere does England take on personality
so strongly as from the sea.*

HILAIRE BELLOC, 'OFF EXMOUTH'

Our Norfolk wherry, the Gipsy, had been laid up for the winter – the winter of 1889 – at Leeuwarden, in Friesland. During two previous summers we had sailed over all the Friesland meres, and made the circuit of the other Netherlands. It was time for us gipsies to move on, and so we cast about to find new cruising grounds.

What we aspired to was, ground not new to ourselves merely, but absolutely fresh waters – if such existed in Europe – accessible to a Norfolk wherry, yet unexplored by any English yacht before.

We studied many maps, and one, a German map on a large scale, disclosed a labyrinth of lakes in Mecklenburg... No English writer had, so far as I could find, dipped pen in ink on the subject. We asked our travelled friends. No one had seen them; few had even heard of them – they lie out of the currents of tourists.

It seemed the very adventure we sought.

But were these unknown lakes get-at-able?

H. M. DOUGHTY, *OUR WHERRY IN WENDISH LANDS: FROM FRIESLAND THROUGH THE MECKLENBURG LAKES, TO BOHEMIA*

There's something about the mobility of a boat – especially a boat you can live on – that appeals to something deep and fundamental inside us. It's the idea that you can just pack up your home and take it with you wherever you want, something that must be connected with our primeval past when we were hunter-gatherers, travelling every day as we followed food, our homes on our backs.

STEVE HAYWOOD, *NARROWBOAT DREAMS*

Surely, surely, slumber is more sweet than toil, the shore
Than labor in the deep mid-ocean, wind and wave and oar;
O, rest ye, brother mariners, we will not wander more.

ALFRED, LORD TENNYSON, FROM 'THE LOTOS-EATERS'

THE TRAVELLER'S REST

I chanced on a hospitable place where the landlord asked if I wanted a bath without implying I badly needed one.

JOHN HILLABY, *JOURNEY THROUGH BRITAIN*

*Of all the beds I ever lay in, that of last night
was the very worst, for there could not be more
than fifty feathers in the bolster and pillow or
double that number in the feather-bed; so there
I lay tossing and turning all night...*

JOHN BYNG, *RIDES ROUND BRITAIN*

*Cities are always best approached at night
when they are at their prettiest and most full of
secrets – especially Arab cities.*

JONATHAN RABAN, *ARABIA*

Pubs Called The Traveller's Rest

Edlesborough, Buckinghamshire
Thornhill, Cardiff
Whitestone, Devon
Brough, Hope Valley, Derbyshire
Talybont-on-Usk, Powys

Hospitality – Take Me To Your Leader

Philoxenia, the love of strangers or hospitality in other words, was central to the ethos of the Ancient Greeks, as to many other ancient cultures. It was one's duty to receive graciously the traveller in a strange land, whatever their quest. The stranger would be welcomed by the leader of the community, offered shelter and protection, food and a bath, before the host asked any questions about his business. This was enforced by the belief that the foreigner might be one of the gods or goddesses travelling in disguise as a test. Offering hospitality to the stranger also ensured the host found out his business; the traveller offered a source of information from the outside world. And it created a bond of friendship between the host and the guest.

Homer's *Odyssey* uses hospitality as a powerful theme, reinforcing the notion that the more civilised a society, the greater the level of hospitality. Odysseus takes the long way home from the Trojan War, his adventures en route to Ithaca taking ten years as he is lured off course, hence an odyssey becoming a byword for a long and meandering voyage. Odysseus' son Telemachus is offered food and shelter at the palace of King Nestor before anyone even asks his name. Odysseus' wife Penelope must offer hospitality to many suitors who believe her husband is dead, even though she wants them to leave; when Odysseus returns, he slays them all, seriously breaching the rules of hospitality. The king of the gods, Zeus, who ruled over the rights of guests, would not have tolerated this, even though it was what the suitors deserved; the goddess Athena must restore his status in the community.

Too many people travel from Hilton to Hilton and think they see the world.

ROBERT KIYOSAKI, AUTHOR OF *RICH DAD, POOR DAD*

No matter how you build it, the motel remains the haunt of the quick and dirty...

WILLIAM LEAST HEAT-MOON, AUTHOR OF
BLUE HIGHWAYS: A JOURNEY INTO AMERICA

'It's funny what a wonderful gentility you get in the bar of a big hotel,' I said.

ERNEST HEMINGWAY, *FIESTA (THE SUN ALSO RISES)*

ROOM SERVICE

Aristotle Onassis said, 'Wherever you go, try to stay at the most famous hotel – even if you can only afford the smallest room!' It's not what everyone aspires to, but many old hotels have a biography that illuminates something of their setting. Even if you don't stay at the Raffles Hotel on Beach Road in Singapore, it would be hard to resist visiting the famous Tiffin Room or the Long Bar. 'Raffles stands for all the fables of the exotic east!' said writer Somerset Maugham. Here are some famous hotels:

Peace Hotel, Shanghai – built in the Gothic style of the Chicago School on the Bund, the colonial and financial centre of old Shanghai overlooking the Huangpu river, was opened as the Cathay Hotel in 1929 by Victor Sassoon, who earned his fortune in opium and arms trading; it became the Peace Hotel in 1956 and is famous for its jazz band.

Waldorf–Astoria, New York – where the US government has rented an entire floor for fifty years; former president Herbert Hoover and retired General Douglas MacArthur lived in suites at one time. Waldorf salad, made with apple, walnuts, celery and mayonnaise (and no Waldorfs at all, Basil Fawlty!), was first created in 1896 by Oscar Tschirky, the maître d'hôtel.

The Ritz Hotel, Piccadilly, London – opened by Swiss hotelier César Ritz, former manager of the Savoy, in 1906; built in a Parisian style over an arcade, its most famous facility is the Palm Court, where Tea at the Ritz has been enjoyed by Charlie Chaplin, Noël Coward, Judy Garland and Queen Elizabeth.

Sandy Lane, St James, Barbados – where the celebrity stories from the 1960s and 1970s are legend: Aristotle Onassis was rowed in from his yacht while Maria Callas swam ashore with a pet marmoset on her back; David Niven invented cocktails at the bar; Elton John adhered to the New Year's Eve black-tie dress code with a black tie around his thigh. The reclusive Greta Garbo felt so comfortable there that she once asked the Dotto boutique to make her a pair of baggy Bermudas, which she wore for the rest of her stay.

La Colombe d'Or, St Paul de Vence, France – the cafe-bar Chez Robinson is how it started out in 1920 below a Provençal hill village; artists used to come and exchange a painting for a few meals or a room, and the walls were soon covered in art. By the time Yves Montand and Simone Signoret were married there, the terrace was adorned with a Léger ceramic, and Miro, Braque and Chagall would all leave their mark, among a growing collection still to be seen in the dining room and the garden.

Fawlty Towers, Torquay – what would you give for a night here, surrounded by the irritable Basil Fawlty played by John Cleese, wife Sybil, waiter Manuel from Barcelona, the deaf Major and all the rest of the mayhem that made Britain's comedy classic (apparently inspired by the Gleneagles Hotel, where the Monty Python team stayed)?

WISH YOU
WEREN'T HERE?

*What the hell had I done? Why
had I come to this awful country?*

WILLIAM SUTCLIFFE, *ARE YOU EXPERIENCED?*

Wales... from curiosity, may be view'd, but it is gloomy, all in dirt and misery, with insolent natives and horrid provisions... In Wales I never saw a flower! They are too lazy to think of them.

JOHN BYNG, *RIDES ROUND BRITAIN*

People... in various stages of exhaustion and expectation, in attitudes of impatience and resignation and despair.

MARGARET DRABBLE DESCRIBES A LONDON AIRPORT IN HER NOVEL *THE RED QUEEN*

BAD TRIPS

Our word 'travel' was first recorded in the late fourteenth century as meaning 'to journey', gradually replacing the Old English *'faran'. Travailen*, 'to make a journey', originally meant 'to toil, labour' as it does in modern-day French. In the Middle Ages, any journey would have been a difficult one, which perhaps explains how the semantic development arose.

PARIS SYNDROME

In 2006, the BBC reported on a strange phenomenon called 'Paris Syndrome' suffered by polite Japanese tourists, a kind of toxic shock from the French capital. Brits may have laughed for years about the rudeness of Parisian waiters, but the stress of having a bad experience in Paris was causing psychiatric breakdown among some of the more starry-eyed seekers of French culture and romance.

Wish someone would appear out of the blue and say, 'I'm really, really sorry, Benedict. The expedition's off.'

BENEDICT ALLEN, *THE SKELETON COAST*

Travels in Dangerous Places

As we've seen, explorers have undertaken dangerous journeys for many reasons over the millennia, often seeking the pot of gold at the end of the rainbow, sometimes literally as they battled the wilderness of the Amazon to find El Dorado or braved the frozen north during the gold rush.

Today, some of those who travel in the most dangerous places are journalists. Christina Lamb, several times Foreign Correspondent of the Year, began her career in Pakistan and travelled the frontiers of Afghanistan when Mujahideen were fighting the Soviet occupiers in the late eighties. Perhaps her most harrowing reporting has been in Zimbabwe, where she went undercover to write a book about the country's plight. David Loyn is a foreign correspondent for the BBC and has travelled with the Taliban on assignment since 9/11. His book *Frontline: Reporting from the World's Deadliest Places* tells the story of many men and women who have risked their lives to bring us the news, so the public can see the true horrors of war.

Once at [Chengdu] airport you are faced with the crush of hundreds, sometimes thousands, of passengers cramped together in a small room, all shouting at the tops of their voices, waving yesterday's boarding passes and ticket stubs at whoever they can. As there is practically permanent fog over Chengdu, flights can be delayed for days... It is here that you learn your first few words of Chinese. No such thing as mañana exists in the vocabulary of these people. Here it is simple *may-oh* which means *no*. It is a wonderful word which occurs with increasing regularity with the more questions you ask...

It is very important not to lose your temper at this stage. I have often laughed at other foreign passengers hopping up and down from one foot to another, slamming the counter with their fists, doing facial impressions of beetroots as they contort themselves in rage.

ALEC LE SUEUR, *THE HOTEL ON THE ROOF*
OF THE WORLD: FIVE YEARS IN TIBET

It is surprising how early one can get up, when camping out. One does not yearn for 'just another five minutes' nearly so much, lying wrapped in a rug on the boards of a boat, with a Gladstone bag for a pillow, as one does in a feather bed.

JEROME K. JEROME, *THREE MEN IN A BOAT*

The Call of the Wild

*Nature halts self-absorption, makes you less
frantic about all that's going on in your
own small mental or physical world.*

MARGARET DRABBLE IN *THE TIMES*

ADVENTURES WITH THE NATURAL WORLD

Whale watching: Vancouver Island, Canada (June through September); Monterey Bay, California; Silver Bank, Dominican Republic (December to April); Kaikoura, New Zealand; Western Cape, South Africa (June to November).

Bush walking: view wildlife and learn the ways of the bush on a walking safari in Africa's game parks: South Luangwa National Park, Zambia; Kruger National Park, South Africa; Selinda Reserve, Botswana.

Horse trekking: spot reindeer and elk by day and relax in the sauna of a log cabin at night on the Bear's Ring Trail, Finland; see the Atlas Mountains, Morocco; or the wild steppes of Mongolia.

How I love this life in the wilderness! I shall never be content to vegetate in England in some quiet country place.

FANNY PARKES, 1884, QUOTED IN *A CORKSCREW IS MOST USEFUL: THE TRAVELLERS OF EMPIRE* BY NICHOLAS MURRAY

MOTHER NATURE

Traci Schauf announced to her husband on the eve of her forty-ninth birthday that she wanted to quit her job and travel, walk and write for one year. She was the primary breadwinner in the family, though two of her children had already left home and the third was in high school: although she had more freedom than ever before, still she worried if she was making the right decision right up until she clicked 'send' on her resignation letter. One co-worker was blunt in her reaction: 'Are you insane?!' But to Traci, the decision 'felt like lightness and freedom'. They had enough savings to get through a few months if they budgeted carefully. Writing about it in *Women's Adventure* magazine, she described it as a moment of reinvention, a 'jump moment'. The result? They spend a week or two every month backpacking and hiking and camping, then go home so Traci can write about it. 'I think everyone can find an activity in the outdoors they enjoy, from reading in a hammock to rock climbing, you just have to go find it. I blog about the things I believe in, like living life outside every chance you get.'

MOMONVACATION.BLOGSPOT.COM

Be careful going in search of adventure – it's ridiculously easy to find.

WILLIAM LEAST HEAT-MOON, AUTHOR OF
BLUE HIGHWAYS: A JOURNEY INTO AMERICA

CAMPING CHECKLIST:

Navigation equipment
Weather protection
Light
First aid kit
Lighter or matches
Food (and cooking utensils if necessary)
Water
Shelter
Knife

I have found a dream of beauty at which one might look all one's life and sigh... A strictly North American beauty – snow splotched mountains, huge pines, red-woods, sugar pines, silver spruce; a crystalline atmosphere, waves of the richest colour; and a pine-hung lake which mirrors all beauty on its surface. Lake Tahoe is before me, a sheet of water twenty-two miles long by ten broad, and in some places 1,700 feet deep. It lies at a height of 6,000 feet and the snow-crowned summits which wall it in are from 8,000 to 11,000 feet in altitude. The air is keen and elastic. There is no sound but the distant and slightly musical ring of the lumberer's axe.

ISABELLA BIRD, 'LAKE TAHOE'

WAYS TO EXPLORE
THE GREAT OUTDOORS:

Walking and hiking

Running

Cycling/mountain biking

Horseback trekking

Cross-country skiing

Camper van

Overlanding

Camel safari

Canoeing or kayaking

White water rafting

Dog-sledding

WALKING WITH TIGERS

Ever wanted to see a tiger in the wild? Satpura National Park, one of India's least-visited parks located in Madhya Pradesh in central India, is a tiger reserve where no more than ten jeeps are allowed inside its 210 square miles at any one time and you can walk in the domain of tigers much as Captain James Forsyth did in the latter part of the nineteenth century. One of the first Europeans to explore the region, he was sent to quell a rebellion in the Satpura jungle, but after walking for 17 miles he found himself at sunset in a lush green plateau with streams to refresh his men. The low-lying hills and peaceful seclusion cast a spell on the British officer, in spite of the menacing wildlife all around: tigers, leopards and bears. He proposed setting up a hill station for British troops, and wrote a book that became a classic, *The Highlands of Central India*. In the same region, a 'wolf child' had been reported found by another British officer a few decades previously; the story so captivated Sir Rudyard Kipling that he visited the region and wrote about it in *The Jungle Book*. Now the national park offers conservation-oriented nature tourism in an area of unspoiled biodiversity. Walking through the jungle allows you to understand it, according to tiger expert Hashim Tyabji, who runs Forsyth's Lodge, a group of cottages built in traditional style. Visitors will see evidence of the tigers all around them, as well as possibly spotting leopard, wild dog and sloth bear, wild ox and parakeets.

'A hyena is stealing our cooler-box,' she whispered urgently.

The sound of a cooler-box being dragged away by a hyena is unmistakable if you've heard it before, which I had.

DICK PITMAN, *A WILD LIFE: ADVENTURES OF AN ACCIDENTAL CONSERVATIONIST IN AFRICA*

Finding Your Feet

Walking expands [the planet] and returns to the walker a sense of its proportions and the intimacy of its appeal to the senses.

CHARLES WILKINS, *WALK TO NEW YORK*

[The journey] took Mr Hamel ten days by horse and would take me, on Shanks's pony, rather more than a month.

SIMON WINCHESTER ON HIS JOURNEY IN *KOREA: A WALK THROUGH THE LAND OF MIRACLES*, A ROUTE THAT TOOK FIFTY MINUTES TO FLY

FREE AS A BIRD

'Why do I become restless after a month in a single place, unbearable after two?'

Bruce Chatwin confessed to restlessness beyond the realms of most of us, something he called 'perpetuum mobile', a need to be moving always. Having walked through Afghanistan and curated an exhibition of nomadic art, he became captivated by the concept of wandering and worked for years on a book he never finished called *The Nomadic Alternative* – though some of its ideas would see the light in his 1987 novel *The Songlines*. At the age of thirty-two, before he became famous, he was staying in rural Oregon in a friend's cabin and walking through the surrounding countryside while he worked on his writing. As revealed in a collection of his letters he wrote to his wife Elizabeth, *Under the Sun*: 'I wandered along the Brown Mountain trail STARK NAKED for 15 miles without coming across a soul but deer and birds.' Dwight Garner, reviewing the collection of letters in *The New York Times*, points out an editor's note in the book, which reveals that a resort caretaker nearby did in fact see him walking, and told the friend who owned the cabin later that he'd seen someone out hiking, naked except for his hiking boots and some flowers tied around his penis.

SHANKS'S PONY

Shanks's pony: one's legs, used as a means of transport. The shank being the lower part of the leg, the term 'Shanks's nag' probably originated in Scotland in the eighteenth century. Some draw a connection with the company Shanks (now Armitage Shanks), which then manufactured lawnmowers; the walker powered the machine by walking with it, like a horse.

In the USA, the expression became 'Shanks's mare', first used there in the 1860s, for example when *The Dubuque Daily Herald* made the erroneous prediction that the bicycle (then a contraption known as a 'velocipede') would 'never come into general use in competition with Shanks's mare' as a mode of transport.

WALKING THE WALL

Mark Thomas, comedian and activist, says one of the best things he's ever done is walk the entire length of the wall that divides Israel and Palestine, an experience he describes in *Extreme Rambling: Walking Israel's Separation Barrier. For Fun.* Talking to people along the 750 kilometres and getting arrested several times mostly for rubbing Israeli checkpoint guards up the wrong way as he crossed from one side to another, he discovered an 'incredibly beautiful landscape' of hills and wild flowers. Thomas has a love of rambling in odd places and believes that through walking you can 'get away from the humdrum nature of your life'.

*There is nothing like walking
to get the feel of a country.*

PAUL SCOTT MOWRER

*I really like that business of setting off
and just walking. I'm pretty sure
that I'll never tire of that.*

BILL BRYSON, INTERVIEWED BY MICHAEL SHAPIRO
IN *A SENSE OF PLACE*

*I discovered a deep contentment brought on by
the world close by and the simplicity of life
on the road; where so many daily trappings
are shed and the air that you breathe and the
ground which you tread become important.*

SPUD TALBOT-PONSONBY, WHO WALKED AROUND
THE COAST OF BRITAIN WITH HER DOG

INSPIRING TRAVELLER: PATRICK LEIGH FERMOR

'If they fall short of the double vision which turns Salisbury Cathedral into Cologne, they invest the scenery with a lustre which is unknown to total abstainers.'

PATRICK LEIGH FERMOR ON THE POTENTIAL BENEFITS
OF HANGOVERS WHILE TRAVELLING

Not long after Patrick Leigh Fermor was born his parents moved to India and left him with another family in Northamptonshire, where he spent a happy three years 'as a wild-natured boy. I wasn't ever told not to do anything'. At school, he resisted academic structure. Expelled when caught holding hands with a local greengrocer's daughter, he educated himself from there on, reading Greek, Latin, Shakespeare and history with hopes of entering Sandhurst.

However, at the age of eighteen he decided instead to walk the length of Europe, 'like a tramp, a pilgrim, or a wandering scholar', from the Hook of Holland to Constantinople (Istanbul). With a longing for freedom and an image of himself as a 'medieval pilgrim, an affable tramp with a knapsack and hobnailed boots', he set off on 8 December 1933 with just a few clothes and books of poetry. He slept in hayricks and shepherds' huts, but also in the castles and country houses of aristocracy. He kept notes and sketches along the way, hoping to write about the journey, but his rucksack was stolen in a youth hostel in Munich, which he saw as something of a blessing for lightening his load, although he lost not only notes but his sleeping bag, money and passport. It was not until forty years after his long walk across Europe that he published *A Time of Gifts* and almost a decade later *Between the Woods and the Water*, describing the events of that time with a wealth of historical, geographical, linguistic and anthropological information – and possibly some creative storytelling.

After his walk he moved to Romania for two years, but in 1939 became a major in Special Operations Executive during World War Two. Living on Crete after the British retreat, he kidnapped the German commander in reprisal for his assault on the villages, events retold in *Ill Met By Moonlight* by his comrade, W. Stanley Moss. In the 1950s, he explored the wild region of the Mani in the southern Peloponnese, where he made his home. At the age of sixty-nine he swam the Hellespont (Dardanelles), the busy strip of water that links the Mediterranean to the Black Sea, in the manner of Lord Byron and many others, including the mythic Leander. He died in June 2011 aged ninety-six.

*O public road, I say back I am not afraid to leave you, yet
I love you,
You express me better than I can express myself,
You shall be more to me than my poem.*

*I think heroic deeds were all conceiv'd in the open air, and all
free poems also,
I think I could stop here myself and do miracles,
I think whatever I shall meet on the road I shall like, and
whoever
beholds me shall like me,
I think whoever I see must be happy.*

WALT WHITMAN, FROM 'SONG OF THE OPEN ROAD'

CAUTIONARY TALES FOR WALKERS

Hilaire Belloc, author of *Cautionary Tales For Children*, was born in 1870 in St Cloud, outside Paris, but grew up in the West Sussex countryside, where began a love of the woods and downs which was to stay with him for the rest of his life. As a boy, he pushed through a beech forest, climbed over a glade 'and I was surprised and glad, because from the ridge of that glade I saw the sea'. It inspired many further walking journeys. He travelled in America, Cuba, France, Spain and the Holy Land, but is known in the walking fraternity for the story of his walk across Sussex, published in 1912 as *The Four Men*, as well as for *The Path to Rome* (1902), an account of his solitary pilgrimage from central France across the Alps and down to Rome, with descriptions of the people and places he encountered, and drawings in pencil and in ink of the route. In *The Hills and the Sea*, he describes some arduous treks through the mountains in France, 'many hours of broken marching and stumbling', and then the moment of hope when he and his companion saw what they believed would be the final scramble to the top of a ridge; at which point, they drank the last of their wine and ate the last of their bread; 'and thus lightened of our provisions, and with more heart in us, we assaulted the final hill...'

You may travel for the sake of great horizons...
and fill your memory with nothing
but views from mountain-tops...

Hilaire Belloc, *Hills and the Sea*

ON THE ROAD

My taxi was furnished like a tart's bedsitter...
done out in what looked like shell-pink mohair.

JONATHAN RABAN, *ARABIA*

I get back on the Triumph and gingerly ease my way out of the services onto the M6. Unused to the immense weight of the luggage on the bike, I squirm between the lanes of motorway traffic... Despite battling with the steering, the amazing, mind-expanding thought is that this road I'm on will eventually take me to Cape Town – the same road these people around me are taking to get to their offices and factories and call centres on this wet October morning.

The adrenalin pumps through my veins, transmits itself through the bars to the forks and the tyres to the tarmac. I may be swaying all over the road like a drunk coming home from a Christmas party, but the road is mine, all mine.

ALAN WHELAN, *AFRICAN BREW-HA-HA*

It is better to travel hopefully than to arrive.

SPANISH PROVERB

The Road goes ever on and on...

J. R. R. TOLKIEN, *LORD OF THE RINGS*

INSPIRING TRAVELLER: CHE GUEVARA

*'Many will call me an adventurer – and that
I am, only one of a different sort.'*

Guevara's 'hunger to explore the world' prompted him to undertake
two long journeys while still a student, which fundamentally
changed his life and that of many others.

In 1950, two years after he began studying medicine at the
University of Buenos Aires, he set out alone on a bicycle on which
he had installed a motor, and toured 2,800 miles around rural
northern Argentina. The following year, he took nine months
to travel almost double that distance with his friend Alberto

Granado. This journey, documented in his book *The Motorcycle Diaries*, took them through much of South America as far as Panama. In Chile, he was enraged by the working conditions of miners and later by the poverty of peasant farmers en route to Machu Picchu, and was moved by an encounter with a penniless couple who were persecuted for being communists. Their journey ended at a leper colony in Peru, on the banks of the Amazon. The motorcycle had broken down by then, and they left aboard a wooden raft. The book was adapted into an award-winning film, which illustrates how what he saw on his journey would inspire his lifelong revolutionary fight to liberate the people of South America. It was in Guatemala, among Cuban exiles, that he acquired his nickname Che, after a common Argentinean manner of speech.

ROAD-TRIPPING

Jack Kerouac's novel *On the Road* was written in 1951, and although fictionalised it is based on his own spontaneous road trips with friends such as Neal Cassady and Allen Ginsberg across America. *The New York Times* hailed it as an icon of the Beat Generation. Kerouac carried small notebooks in which he wrote during the eventful road trips, and he started work on the novel in 1948, based on the first long road trip the year before. Unsatisfied with it, and inspired by a letter from his friend Neal Cassady, in 1950 he decided to tell the story of his years on the road with Cassady as if writing a letter to a friend in a form inspired by improvisational jazz. The first draft was written in three weeks in April 1951 while Kerouac lived in New York, typed single-spaced, without margins or paragraph breaks, on a 120-foot 'scroll' of paper. He continued to revise the manuscript in the coming years, and it was published in 1957. The book was a huge influence on musicians and writers such as Tom Waits, Jim Morrison and Hunter S. Thompson. Bob Dylan said, 'It changed my life like it changed everyone else's.'

TRAVELLERS' TIP – BORDER CROSSINGS

Don't cross any borders in another person's vehicle – if they have any illegal items in their luggage, you will be accountable.

DRIVING ME CRAZY

Proving that it is the travelling and not the arriving that matters, David Treanor tells the epic tale of driving 8,000 miles from England to Mongolia in support of Save the Children in his book *Mission Mongolia: Two Men, One Van. No Turning Back*. He and his pal Geoff were fifty-something BBC radio journalists who grabbed the opportunity of voluntary redundancy and bought an old van to take on an extreme road trip through Ukraine, Russia, Kazakhstan, Siberia and the Gobi. Well, it seemed like a good idea in the pub... Lying in wait are mudslides, mountain tracks and – well, marmots. Geoff learns that if you drive over a dead marmot, the fleas which carry the plague are released into the vehicle's ventilation system. 'Well,' replied David, 'all I can suggest is that we drive round them.'

They Came in Search of Paradise

And all at once they sang, 'Our island home
Is far beyond the wave; we will no longer roam.'

ALFRED, LORD TENNYSON, FROM 'THE LOTOS-EATERS'

South Sea Islands

Kathy Giuffre decided to escape from a stressful life in New Zealand working full-time, and arranged to take a sabbatical in Rarotonga, a tiny speck in the middle of the South Pacific. At the last minute, her boyfriend backed out, leaving her to travel the 11,000 kilometres alone with her two young children to a place where she knew no one. Her account of this extraordinary time, *An Afternoon in Summer*, is an inspirational book about searching for, and ultimately finding, a better life.

Many of the most famous works of art by Paul Gauguin are from the South Pacific island of Tahiti. Gauguin, in 1890, was ready to escape from life in Europe. A letter from his friend Émile Bernard responded in kind: 'Oh to leave without having to worry about anything, far far away. To leave the abominable life... its boors, its layabouts, its moaners, this plague-stricken breed.'

The following year, as Rosie Millard explains in *Bonnes Vacances*, Gauguin wrote to the French Minister of Fine Arts:

'I would like to go to Tahiti to make a series of paintings to capture the character and light of this country. Sir, I have the honour of requesting that you grant me official creditation... which although unsalaried would nevertheless, by the advantages it would proffer, facilitate my studies...'

Having received this swiftly, he made up his mind:

'... in a little while I shall go to Tahiti, a small island in Oceania, where material life can be lived without money [...] Out there, beneath a winterless sky, on marvellously fertile soil, the Tahitian need only lift up his arms to pick his food; for that reason, he never works. In Europe, however, men and women can satisfy their needs only by toiling without respite...'

Of course it was not quite like that, although his paintings indeed do depict Tahiti as a form of paradise.

IN SEARCH OF SHANGRI-LA

Shangri-La is a fictional place depicted in the 1933 novel *Lost Horizon* by British author James Hilton: a mystical, harmonious valley hidden in the western end of the Kunlun Mountains. Shangri-La has become interchangeable with any earthly paradise – an isolated utopia concealed from modern man. The narrative describes inhabitants who live years beyond the normal lifespan and only age in appearance very slowly. Many have tried to find 'the real Shangri-La'. It is often suggested that James Hilton took his inspiration from the green Hunza Valley in northern Pakistan, close to the Tibetan border, which he visited a few years before the book was published. Bhutan, with its unique form of Tibetan Buddhism and relative isolation from the outside world, has been dubbed the last Shangri-La.

INSPIRING TRAVELLER: EDWARD LEAR

*'When have I not been weary in winter time,
or indeed anywhere when settled?'*

Born in 1812, Lear is best known today for his nonsense poems and limericks, but he was also an artist, illustrator and poet. He was the twenty-first child of Ann and Jeremiah Lear and from the age of six he suffered frequent health problems including epileptic seizures and depression, which he later referred to as 'the Morbids'.

However, he travelled widely throughout his life, and before and after the publication of the *Book of Nonsense*, he also published his journals as a landscape painter, showing vividly in drawings and paintings the places he travelled: Italy, Greece, Corsica and Albania. Queen Victoria was pleased by his *Illustrated Excursions in Italy* and summoned him to court, where he gave her drawing lessons. As well as the Mediterranean, where he was drawn to the strong sunlight and intense colour, he also toured India and Ceylon in 1873–75. He produced coloured wash drawings on the road, which he then worked into oils and watercolours back in his studio.

Eventually, he settled in San Remo, on his beloved Mediterranean coast, at a villa he named Villa Tennyson, with his Suliot chef, Giorgis (a faithful friend and, as Lear complained, a thoroughly unsatisfactory chef), and his cat, Foss.

As a writer, one of my themes – maybe the theme of my life – is about the constant search for somewhere new, somewhere better.

LAURIE GOUGH

Most of my treasured memories of travel are recollections of sitting.

ROBERT THOMAS ALLEN

20 GREAT TRAVEL FILMS TO GET YOU DREAMING:

The Beach	*Thelma and Louise*
Lost in Translation	*French Kiss*
Into the Wild	*The Darjeeling Limited*
The Motorcycle Diaries	*The Constant Gardener*
Outsourced	*Run Lola Run*
In Bruges	*Breakfast at Tiffany's*
Sideways	*Fear and Loathing in Las Vegas*
Monsoon Wedding	*Goodbye Lenin*
Kundun	*Roman Holiday*
Swimming to Cambodia	*Vicky Cristina Barcelona*

A Mediterranean Idyll

Percy Bysshe Shelley (1792–1822) loved Italy, bathing in Mediterranean coves, sailing in Venice or watching the changing weather in the Apennines while reading the Ancient Greeks. At the age of twenty-six he moved there and lived there for the last four years of his short life. He said of the Italian landscape, of skies, trees, mountains and sea:

'I depend on these things for life, for in the smoke of cities and the tumult of human kind and the chilling fogs of our own country I can scarcely be said to live.'

Once again, I'm alone with the geckos and my many hidden detractors – living creatures that crawl and creep soundlessly in the undergrowth, observing my every move. I pop my shades back on and stride out into the sun, the insecure owner of a partially restored pile in a foreign country. Here, in the craggy north-west mountains of Mallorca, I feel light-years away from my flat in central London with the shuddering, creaky cabs passing my windows and the constant judder of coaches and lorries as they thunder by, night and day. The air is still and fragrant and the lisping cicadas with their monotone pulsating beat lure me into a state of momentary calm.

ANNA NICHOLAS, *A LIZARD IN MY LUGGAGE*

WHEN IN ROME...

*If you reject the food, ignore the customs,
fear the religion and avoid the people,
you might better stay at home.*

JAMES MICHENER

Travellers' Tips – Local Customs and Traditions

✈ The foot is considered a low and unclean part of the
body in Thailand and other parts of Asia, so pointing
your feet towards someone is disrespectful – it's
especially bad form to point your feet towards a
Buddha statue in a temple, or towards anyone in a
public place, or to put your feet up on a table or
chair. If you accidentally do this, you can apologise
by touching your hand to the person's arm and then
touching your own head. It can also be deemed a little
overly familiar to touch someone you don't know well
on their head, which is spiritually the highest part of
the body.

✈ In Nepal, it is bad manners to step over someone's
outstretched legs, and likewise you should not leave
your legs outstretched when someone wants to pass.

✈ In Middle Eastern culture, it was traditionally considered correct to take care of strangers and foreigners. The bond was formed by eating salt under one's roof, and was so strict that an Arab story tells of a thief who tasted something to see if it was sugar, and on realising it was salt, put back all that he had taken and left.

One can only really travel if one lets oneself go and takes what every place brings...

FREYA STARK

'Tell me – do you or do you not eat the body and blood of the big white Chief of your tribe once every seven days...?'

REDMOND O'HANLON, *CONGO JOURNEY*, BEING QUESTIONED
ABOUT HIS DOUBLE STANDARDS REGARDING CANNIBALISM

LOCAL FESTIVALS

Festival of Snakes – on 19 March, St Joseph's Day, in Cocullo, Abruzzo, the villagers capture snakes from the nearby hills, which they will later release back into the wild; they have been 'taming the snakes' since 700 BC.

Berlin's Love Parade – in the first week in July, the biggest street party in the world takes place in Berlin, with everyone dressed in as little as possible; like Rio Carnival with a strange twist.

The Baby Jumping Festival – in the second week in June in Castrillo de Murcia, Spain, local people continue a tradition dating from 1620 to celebrate Corpus Christi by dressing as the Devil and leaping over a row of babies, in a ritual said to cleanse them of sin and protect them against evil spirits in the future.

Boryeong Mud Festival – every July, people descend on the ten million metres of mud in Boryeong, South Korea, known for its cleansing and healing properties; you cover yourself in it and go from mud bath to mud wrestling and mud massage.

Calgary Stampede – the first two weeks of July in this Canadian city in view of the Rockies see live country music, bucking broncos and a lot of Stetsons.

Day of the Dead – this two-day festival from 1 November in Oaxaca, Mexico, features a parade of skeletons on stilts taking flowers to a cemetery, accompanied by mariachi bands and sugar skulls.

Dragon Boat Festival – on the fifth day of the fifth lunar month (June), the Chinese honour Qu Yuan, poet and adviser to the emperor, with races in long canoes shaped like dragons.

AN OUTSIDE PERSPECTIVE

Jehangeer Nowrojee and Hirjeebhoy Merwanjee went to England to apprentice themselves to shipbuilders and bring back the latest techniques to India. Published in 1841, *Journal of a Residence of Two Years and a Half in Great Britain*, is their account of their stay in Britain. They were astonished by the number of carriages of different descriptions in London, and amused by the drivers of hackney cabs:

'It is very amusing to those who know London well to see how cunning and knowing the drivers of these vehicles look, when a stranger directs them to drive to any place not more than a few yards distance. Their thumb is placed to their nose and a twirl of their outstretched fingers announces to their brethren that they have "caught a flat", to use their own words...'

One of the things that amazed them most was the adulation poured on a much feted French dancer:

'... to us it appeared of very little interest; and we were very much surprised to hear that for every night that she had appeared upon the stage she had been paid one hundred and fifty guineas!! It does appear so absurd that a dancing woman should thus take out of English pockets every night, for an hour's jumping, more than would keep six weavers of silk, their wives and families, for

a whole year. Had we not seen instances that convinced us the English were clever people, we should have thought them very foolish indeed thus to pay a dancing puppet.'

Travel is a violation of the natural order, or at least that's what the Saramaka believe.

JOHN GIMLETTE, *WILD COAST*

LIVING WITH THE PEOPLE OF THE POLAR NORTH

'From the earliest boyhood I played and worked with the hunters, so even the hardships of the most strenuous sledge-trips became pleasant routine for me.'

Knud Johan Victor Rasmussen was born in 1879 in Greenland, son of a Danish missionary and an Inuit-Danish mother. From a young age he learned to speak the Inuit language and to drive dog sleds in Arctic conditions. After returning to Denmark for his education (he failed to graduate from university, and had a brief stint as an actor and opera singer), he participated in his first expedition and as a result wrote *The People of the Polar North* in 1908, a travel journal and scholarly account of Inuit culture. With a friend, he set up the Thule Trading Station in Uummannaq as a base for future expeditions to learn about the language and culture of the region. His greatest achievement was the Fifth Thule Expedition (1921–24), an investigation into the origins of the 'Eskimo' race. He not only collected many volumes of data on folklore and language, and artefacts still on display in Denmark, documenting practically every tribe of Inuit, but in the course of his travels became the first European to cross the Northwest Passage via dog sled, travelling for more than 18,000 kilometres over sixteen months with Inuit hunters across North

America from Hudson Bay to the Bering Sea; he would have continued to Russia but his visa was refused, so he returned to translate his findings, write and give lectures. The ethnographer, known as the 'father of Eskimology', died at the age of fifty-four of pneumonia after a bout of food poisoning.

WE COME IN PEACE

Robert Macfarlane, in *Mountains of the Mind*, tells of how on his first expedition to Greenland, one particular explorer brought with him a flag on which was painted an olive branch, hoping to convince the native people that he came in peace. It had not occurred to him that the accepted symbolism of the olive branch might not have reached the people of Greenland, 'who lived in an ice world almost entirely devoid of vegetation, let alone of trees.'

MAD DOGS AND ENGLISHMEN: CRAZY ADVENTURES

*Believe me! The secret of reaping the greatest
fruitfulness and the greatest enjoyment
from life is to live dangerously!*

FRIEDRICH NIETZSCHE

CYCLING TO THE ASHES

'Every day something fantastic happened.'

On October 2009, Oli Broom left Lord's Cricket Ground in London on his bicycle along with seventeen friends. When they reached the south coast, his friends went home again, but Oli took a ferry across to France and continued cycling. His aim was to cycle to the Ashes in Brisbane, Australia in November the following year, and he carried a cricket bat so he could stop and have a game wherever he went. The journey, which took him 25,000 kilometres, raised £30,000 for his chosen charities, the British Neurological Research Trust and the Lord's Taverners.

WWW.CYCLINGTOTHEASHES.COM

THE MAN WHO SWAM THE AMAZON

In February 2008, Slovenian Martin Strel – who taught himself to swim in a stream at the age of six – began a swim down the Amazon. 'The Fishman' had already swum the Adriatic Sea, across the Mediterranean from Tunisia to Italy, the Danube from source to estuary, the Mississippi and the Yangtze; although a record-breaking marathon swimmer, he was middle-aged and no athlete. Over sixty-six days, he swam 3,274 miles down the world's deadliest river from Atalaya in Peru to Belém on the Atlantic coast of Brazil, almost killing himself in the process, raising awareness for the plight of the Amazon rainforest and for peace and clean water everywhere. The whole world followed his achievement, recorded in an award-winning film, *Big River Man*, and a book, *The Man Who Swam the Amazon*. He took a break after that to travel the world and speak to people about his adventures and the causes he believes in.

WWW.AMAZONSWIM.COM

NATURAL HIGHS AND LOWS

Maya Gabeira rode the biggest wave ever surfed by a woman at Dungeons in South Africa, 45 feet high

Bonita Norris at twenty-two became the youngest British woman to climb Mount Everest

Edurne Pasaban was the first woman to climb all of the world's fourteen highest mountains

Freediver Sara Campbell was the first woman to hit 90 metres depth while using only her monofin to descend

ADAPTED FROM *THE INDEPENDENT ON SUNDAY*

Board Free

Dave Cornthwaite's wanderlust began in Uganda, when a gap year teaching scheme organised by Africa & Asia Venture encouraged a passion for pastures new. While at university, he hitchhiked to Morocco for charity. Then in April 2005, he left behind a job as a graphic designer, and started to plan two world record-breaking journeys. In 2006 he pushed his longboard (skateboard) from John O'Groats to Land's End, becoming the first person to skate the length of Britain. The following year he completed a five-month 5,823-kilometre skate across Australia from Perth to Brisbane. Smitten by the bug, he launched Expedition1000, a series of twenty-five journeys, each at least 1,000 miles in length and using a different method of non-motorised transport each time. In April 2011 he finished a 1,400-mile tandem bicycle ride in fourteen days between Vancouver, BC and Las Vegas, Nevada.

WWW.DAVECORNTHWAITE.COM

INSPIRING TRAVELLER: FREYA STARK

'To awaken quite alone in a strange town is one of the pleasantest sensations in the world.'

FREYA STARK

Freya Madeline Stark was born on 31 January 1893 in Paris, where her parents were studying art. Her mother was Italian of Polish–German descent, and her father was English from Devon, and she grew up in England and Italy. At the age of nine she received a copy of *One Thousand and One Nights* and became fascinated with the Orient. Often ill while young, she escaped into books and enjoyed learning languages.

After working as a nurse in Italy during World War One, she continued her education at the School of Oriental Studies in London. Then in 1927, she boarded a ship for Beirut, intent on travelling and exploring.

Basing herself in Lebanon and then Baghdad, by 1931 she had completed three hazardous treks into the wilderness of western Iran (then Persia) and located the fabled Valleys of the Assassins, on which her first major book was based. She continued into southern Arabia and the Middle East, later in Afghanistan and Nepal. In World War Two she worked for the British Ministry of Information in Aden, Baghdad and Cairo.

The travels were recorded in twenty-four highly personal books acclaimed for their sense of history and culture, including practical advice alongside entertaining descriptions of people and everyday life. She was the first westerner to travel through much of the Middle East, one of the first Western women to explore the Arabian deserts, and in spite of a lifetime of dangerous journeys, she died in Italy at the age of 100.

It would be the experience of a lifetime, good or bad, and I would never forget it.

MARIE TIÈCHE, *CHAMPAGNE AND POLAR BEARS: ROMANCE IN THE ARCTIC*

THE WRONG WAY ROUND

'... the first time I went out on my own the hardest thing I dealt with was the loneliness,' said Briton Dee Caffari, who became the only woman to have sailed non-stop around the world three times at the age of thirty-eight. 'Everyone assumes I grew up in dinghies, but actually I grew up in ballet shoes and tap shoes.' Her father loved the sea and kept a motorboat on the Thames, but she didn't sail until she went to university. She started out working as a PE teacher, but retrained a couple of years later as a water sports instructor. After watching the start of the 2001 Global Challenge race, in 2004 she entered as skipper. She was the first woman to sail solo around the world the 'wrong' way – against the prevailing winds – in 2006, and the first woman to circumnavigate the world non-stop in both directions.

Could YOU ski to the South Pole?

That was the challenge that adventurer Felicity Aston, who had spent three years working in the Antarctic, put to women from around the Commonwealth, hoping to create the most international all-female expedition ever to the Pole. She didn't want experienced explorers but 'ordinary' women with a desire to inspire others to follow their dreams. She received more than 800 applications. 'What is skiing?' asked someone in Ghana. At the close of 2009, Felicity led a team from places as diverse as Jamaica, India, Singapore and Cyprus – some of whom had never even seen snow or spent the night in a tent before joining the expedition – on one of the toughest journeys on the planet. Eighty-mile-an-hour winds ripped through base camp; frostbite and injuries were an everyday occurrence; deadly crevasses cracked beneath their feet. But they also shared beliefs, ideas, philosophies – and laughter. And they made it back to tell the tale.

WWW.FELICITYASTON.CO.UK

I inquired of all my friends as a beginning what they knew of West Africa. The majority knew nothing. A percentage said, 'Oh, you can't possibly go there; that's where Sierra Leone is, the white man's grave, you know.'

MARY KINGSLEY, *TRAVELS IN WEST AFRICA*

ROWING SOLO

Perhaps the most important thing Sarah Outen took with her in April 2009, when at the age of twenty-three she embarked on a solo voyage across the Indian Ocean in her rowing boat, *Dippers*, was 500 Mars bars. Food became a constant obsession after her 'land food' ran out, and discovering fairly early on that powdered food wasn't a good substitute when you are burning so many calories rowing day and night, she constantly delved into the stores to find what surprises lurked there. Over the course of 4,000 miles of unpredictable ocean, over 124 days, powered by grief for the loss of her father and a determination to live life to the full, Sarah negotiated wild ocean storms, unexpected encounters with whales and the continuous threat of being capsized by passing container ships. She lost 20 kilograms of body weight before arriving in Mauritius, where she became the first woman and the youngest person to row solo across the Indian Ocean. In 2011, she set out to circumnavigate the globe by her own power.

WWW.SARAHOUTEN.COM

MAD WHITE GIANT

In 1983, at the age of twenty-three, Benedict Allen crossed the remote rainforest between the Orinoco and the Amazon, resulting in his first book, *Mad White Giant*. Following this, he went through a six-week initiation ceremony in Papua New Guinea, described in *Into the Crocodile Nest*. Other expeditions have included a search for an apeman in Sumatra, a trek through Australia's Gibson Desert, and a 3,600-mile journey across the Amazon Basin, *Through Jaguar Eyes*. Several of his expeditions were recorded for the BBC, including his journey with bad-tempered camels through Namibia, *The Skeleton Coast* – the first time the journey had been permitted by any government of Namibia – immersing himself in the ways of the nomadic Himba people. He tries to learn skills from the indigenous peoples to help him cope with extraordinary conditions.

'Bite from camel,' says one entry in the death columns of the Windhoek Archives from a hundred years ago.

BENEDICT ALLEN, *THE SKELETON COAST*

Parting Thoughts: Souvenirs

I believe that bringing home a broader perspective is the best souvenir.

Rick Steves

One's destination is never a place,
but a new way of seeing things.

HENRY MILLER

The world is a book and those who
do not travel read only one page.

ST AUGUSTINE

*Like all great travellers, I have seen more
than I remember, and remember
more than I have seen.*

BENJAMIN DISRAELI

He who goes everywhere gains everywhere.

FRENCH PROVERB

No one realises how beautiful it is to travel until he comes home and rests his head on his old, familiar pillow.

LIN YUTANG

... the joyful jump on English soil – the rail-carriage, second class – the cab – the knock at the door – the tumbling up stairs... the first glass of London stout!'

SIR RICHARD BURTON

*Stop worrying about the potholes in
the road and celebrate the journey.*

FITZHUGH MULLAN

*Without new experiences, something inside
of us sleeps. The sleeper must awaken.*

FRANK HERBERT

*We find after years of struggle that we
do not take a trip; a trip takes us.*

JOHN STEINBECK

*Our own inner minds and consciousness, not
other people's lands, are the final frontier.*

BENEDICT ALLEN, *THE SKELETON COAST*

RESOURCES

Murray, Nicholas *A Corkscrew is Most Useful: The Travellers of Empire* (2008, Abacus)

Shapiro, Michael *A Sense of Place* (2004, Travelers' Tales)

Stone, Jon R. *Routledge Book of World Proverbs* (2006, Routledge)

Robinson, Jillian *Change Your Life Through Travel* (2006, Footsteps Media)

Traveller magazine

Wanderlust magazine

www.summersdale.com